DRAWING NEAR TO GOD
MY PORTION FOREVER

Where can the soul be better than in drawing near to God?
—Thomas Watson.

DRAWING NEAR TO GOD MY PORTION FOREVER

By
Thomas Boston
Jonathan Edwards
George Swinnock
William Guthrie
Hugh Binning
Thomas Watson
Richard Sibbes

Minneapolis

Published by Curiosmith.
Minneapolis, Minnesota.
Internet: curiosmith.com.

The text of "Of Man's Chief End and Happiness" by THOMAS BOSTON is from *An Illustration of the Doctrines of the Christian Religion, with Respect to Faith and Practice, Upon the Plan of the Assembly's Shorter Catechism; Comprehending a Complete Body of Divinity*. Aberdeen: George and Robert King, 1848.

The text of "God the Best Portion of the Christian" by Jonathan Edwards is from *The Works of Jonathan Edwards, A.M.*, Vol., 2, revised and corrected by Edward Hickman. London: Ball, Arnold, and Co., 1840.

The text of "God Is a Satisfying Portion" By George Swinnock is from *The works of George Swinnock, M.A.*, Vol. 4. Edinburgh: James Nichol, 1868.

The text of "It Is Good for Me to Draw Near to God" by William Guthrie is from *A Collection of Lectures and Sermons*, Sermon I, Psalm 73:28. Kilmarnock: Joseph Graham and Co., 1809.

The text of "It Is Good to Draw Near to God" by Hugh Binning is from *The Works of The Rev. Hugh Binning, M.A.*, Heart Humiliation Sermon 5. Edinburgh, London and Dublin: A. Fullarton and Co., 1851.

The text of "The Happiness of Drawing Near to God" by Thomas Watson is from *The Christian Soldier or Heaven Taken by Storm, etc.*, Rev. Mr. Armstrong editor. New York: Robert Moore, 1816.

The text of "The Saint's Happiness" by Richard Sibbes is from *The Complete Works of Richard Sibbes, D.D.*, Vol. 7, edited by Rev. Alexander Grosart. Edinbough: James Nichol, 1844. Footnotes marked G. are from Rev. Grosart.

Elizabethan verbs and pronouns are updated to modern English word for word.

King James Bible text quotations are left as is.

The "Guide to the Contents" was added to this edition by the publisher.

Supplementary content, compilation, book layout, and cover design: Copyright © 2018 Charles J. Doe

ISBN 9781946145406

GUIDE TO THE CONTENTS

1. Of Man's Chief End and Happiness by Thomas Boston. . . . 11
    I. The glorifying of God, part of man's chief end. . . . 12
        1. The nature of glorifying God: heart, lips and life. . . . 12
        2. The respects God's glory is man's chief end. . . . 14
        3. The extent of glorifying God: natural, civil, moral and religious actions. . . . 16
        4. The reason is because he is the first principle, he must be the last end. . . . 18
    II. The enjoyment of God forever, man's chief happiness. . . . 18
        1. The nature of enjoyment: imperfect and perfect. . . . 19
        2. The order: glorifying God comes before enjoyment of God. . . . 20
        3. The enjoyment of God is man's chief end in point of happiness: what man is and what God is. . . . 21
    III. Concluding inferences. . . . 22
        1. Sin perverts the spirit, turning it from its chief end. . . . 22
        2. God is dishonored by our hearts, lips, and lives. . . . 22
        3. Men turn slaves to that which was made to serve him. . . . 23
        4. The soul of man is immortal and his happiness must be in the immortal God. . . . 23
        5. When God and the creature come in competition, we must renounce the creature. . . . 24
        6. Doctrine that glorifies God is from God. . . . 24
        7. The main work is to glorify God and to enjoy him. . . . 25

2. God the Best Portion of the Christian by Jonathan Edwards. . . . 26
    I. A godly man prefers God before anything else in heaven. . . . 27
        1. He prefers God before anything else that actually is in heaven. . . . 27
        2. He prefers God before anything else that might be in heaven. . . . 29
    II. A godly man prefers God before all other things on the earth. . . . 30
        1. The saint prefers enjoyment of God to anything in this world. . . . 30
        2. The saint prefers what of God may be obtained in this life before all things in the world. . . . 30
        3. The saint prefers what he has already of God before anything in this world: possessions, prospects, and conceptions. . . . 32
    III. Application. . . . 33
        1. Whatever changes a godly man passes through, he is happy, because God, is his chosen portion. . . . 33
        2. Examine yourself whether you prefer God above all things—five questions. . . . 34
        3. Two sure ways to determine what you prefer. . . . 37

3. The Attributes of God As Our Portion by George Swinnock. . . . 40
    I. God is a satisfying portion. . . . 40
    II. God is a sanctifying ennobling portion. . . . 46
    III. God is universal portion. . . . 49
    IV. God is an eternal portion. . . . 52

GUIDE TO THE CONTENTS *(Continued)*

    V. God is a comforting portion. . . . 58
        1. God is a comfort against the death of our friends. . . . 60
        2. God is a comfort against your own death. . . . 61

4. It Is Good for Me to Draw Near to God by William Guthrie. . . . 66
    I. Consider the text simply or absolutely. . . . 66
        1. What it is to draw near unto God: 1.) Make peace with God, 2.) Seek more after fellowship with God, and 3.) Make sure of your peace with God. . . . 67
        2. What are the advantages of drawing near to God: 1.) It is good in itself and a pleasant good, and 2.) It is a creditable, honorable and profitable good. . . . 69
    II. Consider the words that reference what goes before in the text. . . . 74
        1. He had seen the wicked prosper and he stumbled but then considers: 1.) Satisfaction of a gaining of God, and 2.) The people of God should still draw near unto God. . . . 74
        2. Although a man be near unto God, it is good to seek more intimate acquaintance with God. . . . 77
        3. The only way to secure a man from the dreadful judgments is to draw near to God. . . . 79

5. It Is Good for Me to Draw Near to God by Hugh Binning. . . . 81
    I. The first step and degree of union with God—faith in Jesus Christ. . . . 82
    II. The commendation of "It is good." . . . 84
    III. There is nothing more practicable than the life of religion. . . . 86
    IV. That which all men seek after is happiness and well-being. . . . 87
    V. Know wherein the true well-being and eternal welfare of our souls consist. . . . 88
    VI. Drawing near to God, commendation and application. . . . 89

6. The Happiness of Drawing Near to God by Thomas Watson. . . . 94
    I. By nature we are far from God. . . . 95
    II. It is a great duty incumbent upon Christians to draw near to God. . . . 96
        1. How we are capable of drawing near to God. . . . 97
        2. Where we draw near to God. . . . 98
        3. The manner of our drawing near to God. . . . 98
        4. Why we must draw near to God. . . . 98
    III. God is the chief good. . . . 99
        1. A gracious soul is ever drawing near to God. . . . 99
        2. It reproves them who draw near to the world. . . . 100
        3. It reproves them who draw near with their lips but not hearts. . . . 101
        4. It reproves them who draw back from God. . . . 102
        5. It exhorts us all to draw near to God. . . . 102
    IV. Two motives for drawing near to God. . . . 102
        1. It is a good thing: wisdom, honor, safety, peace, and riches. . . . 102
        2. In the future we shall wish we had drawn near to God. . . . 105

GUIDE TO THE CONTENTS *(Continued)*

    V. How shall we do to draw near to God? . . . 105

7. The Saint's Happiness by Richard Sibbes. . . . 108
    I. *First*, God's dearest children are exercised with sharp conflicts in the faith of principles, yea, of God's providence. . . . 109
    II. *Second*, God's children, though they be thus low, yet they shall recover. . . . 109
    III. *Third*, The way for a Christian to recover his ground in time of temptation, is for him to enter into God's sanctuary. . . . 109
    IV. *Fourth*, Whether it be the eye of faith or the eye of sense, all serves to bring us nearer to God. . . . 110
    V. *Fifth*, That the course of the children of God is a course contrary to the stream of the world. . . . 110
    VI. *Sixth*, That God's Spirit enables his children by experience to justify wisdom. . . . 111
    VII. *Seventh*, Spiritual conviction is the ground of practice. . . . 114
    VIII. *Eighth*, Man's happiness is in communion with God. . . . 117
    Use 1. Teach us how to think on God as a Father. . . . 119
    Use 2. Labor for more full participation of his Spirit. . . . 120
        1. Labor to be conversant in spiritual means. . . . 120
        2. Converse with those that draw near unto him. . . . 120
        3. Be much in prayer. . . . 121
        4. Check the first motions of sin in our hearts. . . . 121
        5. Be in God's walks and ordinances in a coarse of doing good. . . . 123
        6. Observe God's dealings with the church. . . . 123
        7. Labor to maintain humility. . . . 124
        8. Labor for sincerity in all our actions. . . . 124
        9. Observe the first motions of God's Spirit. . . . 125
        10. Take up daily controversies that do arise in us, through the inconstancy of our deceivable hearts. . . . 125
    Use 3. Instruction. . . . 126
        1. A Christian that thus draws near to God is the wisest man. . . . 126
        2. Learn how to justify zeal in religion. . . . 126
        3. A man must not break with God for any creature's sake whatever. . . . 127
    Use 4. Use of trial to know whether we draw near to God or not. . . . 127
        1. A further desire of increase of communion with God. . . . 127
        2. In abasing or humbling ourselves. . . . 128
        3. The nearer we are to God, the more we admire heavenly things. . . . 128
        4. When we have a sense and sight of sin, then we may truly be said to draw near. . . . 128
        5. The nearer we draw to God, the more is our rest. . . . 129
        6. Those that draw near to God will fly to him with confidence. . . . 129
        7. He that is near to God is neither afraid of God nor of any creature. . . . 129
        8. The nearer we are to God, the more in love we will be with spiritual exercises. . . . 130
        9. He will stand against opposition, and that out of experience. . . . 130

*Whom have I in heaven but thee? and there is none upon earth that I desire beside thee. My flesh and my heart faileth: but God is the strength of my heart, and my portion for ever. For, lo, they that are far from thee shall perish: thou hast destroyed all them that go a whoring from thee. But it is good for me to draw near to God: I have put my trust in the Lord G*OD*, that I may declare all thy works.—*PSALM 73:25-28 (KJV).

Sermon 1

OF MAN'S CHIEF END AND HAPPINESS

By Thomas Boston

Whether therefore ye eat or drink, or whatsoever ye do, do all to the glory of God.—1 Corinthians 10:31.

Whom have I in heaven but thee? and there is none upon earth that I desire besides thee. My flesh and my heart faileth: but God is the strength of my heart, and my portion for ever. —Psalm 73:25, 26.

Knowledge is a necessary foundation of faith and holiness; and where ignorance reigns in the mind, there is confusion in the heart and life. We have the word of truth in our hands, and many methodical systems of divine truths, amongst which the Shorter Catechism, composed by the Reverend Assembly of Divines at Westminster, in pursuance of the solemn league and covenant, as a part of the then intended uniformity between the three nations, is deservedly reckoned the chief. This I shall endeavor to explain with all possible brevity and perspicuity, that you may have a view of those divine truths, with the reasons of them. And this I have thought it the more necessary to do, in order that your minds may be established in the truth, as our time is like to be a time of trial, wherein you may be exposed to many snares, and so be in danger of apostasy.

In the first of the texts which I have read, you have,

1. The chief end of human actions, the glory of God: that is the scope of which all we think, or speak, or do, should tend; this is the point or common center, in which all should meet.

2. The extent of it. It is not only some of our actions, but all of them, of what kind soever, that must be directed to this end. This, then, is man's chief duty.

In the second text we have,

1. The Psalmist's chief desire, and what he points at as his only true happiness; that is, the enjoyment of God. He takes God for and instead of all, that in him alone his soul may rest.

2. The reason of this is taken from, (1.) The creature's emptiness, both in body and spirit, verse 25. (2.) From God's fullness and sufficiency: and this is amplified by the eternity of it, *my portion for ever.*

From both texts the following doctrine natively follows.

DOCTRINE. "Man's chief end is to glorify God, and to enjoy him for ever."

In handling this doctrine, I shall speak,

I. To the glorifying of God, which is one part of man's chief end.

II. To the enjoyment of God for ever, wherein man's chief happiness consists, and which he is to seek as his chief good.

I. I shall speak to the glorifying of God, which is one part of man's chief end. And here I shall show,

1. The nature of glorifying God.
2. In what respects God's glory is man's chief end.
3. The extent of this glorifying God.
4. The reason of it.

FIRST, I shall show the nature of glorifying God. To glorify, is either to make glorious, or to declare to be glorious. God glorifies, *i.e.* makes angels or men glorious; but man cannot make God glorious, for he is not capable of any additional glory, being in himself infinitely glorious.[1] Hence it is plain, that God gets no advantage to himself by the best works of men, the profit of our holiness redounding entirely to ourselves.[2]

God is glorified, then, only declaratively; he is glorified when his glory is declared. This is done two ways. Objectively, by the creatures inanimate and irrational. Thus the heavens declare the glory of God.[3] This the creatures do, while they afford matter of praise to God, as a violin is fit to make music, though there must be a hand to play on it ere it can sound. Man declares his glory also actively. And this he ought to do,

1. By his heart, "Glorify God in your spirit."[4] Honoring God with the lips, not with the heart, is but a very lame and unacceptable performance. He ought to be glorified by our understanding, taking him up in the glory which the Scripture reveals him in, thinking highly of him, and esteeming him above all other persons or things.[5] So they that know him not, can never glorify him: and they that esteem any person or thing more than, or as much as him, dishonor him. We glorify him by our wills, choosing him as our portion and chief good, as he really is in himself; by our affections loving him, and rejoicing and delighting in him above every other.

2. By his lips, "Whoso offereth praise glorifieth me."[6] Therefore man's tongue is called his glory,[7] not only because

---

1 Job 35:7.
2 Acts 17:25; Psalm 16:2.
3 Psalm 19:1.
4 1 Corinthians 6:20.
5 Psalm 73:25.
6 Psalm 50:23.
7 Psalm 16:9.

it serves him for speech, which exalts him above the brutes, but because it is given him as a proper instrument for speaking forth the glory of God. So that it must needs be a strange perverting of the tongue, to set it against the heavens, and let it loose to the dishonor of God, and fetter it as to his glory.

3. By his life. "Let your light so shine before men, that they may see your good works, and glorify your Father which is in heaven."[1] A holy life is a life of light; it is a shining light, to let a blind world see the glory of God. Sin darkens the glory of God, draws a veil over it. David's sin made the enemies of the Lord to blaspheme. The study of holiness says, God is holy; mourning for every slip says, God is spotless; walking holily in all manner of conversation, within and without, etc. says, God is omniscient and omnipresent, etc. As when men find a well-ordered family, that tells what a man the master of it is.

SECONDLY, I proceed to show in what respects God's glory is man's chief end.

First, It is man's end,

1. It is the end which God aimed at when he made man. "The Lord hath made all things for himself."[2] "For of him, and through him, and to him are all things."[3] Every rational agent proposes to himself an end in working, and the most perfect the highest end. Now God is the most perfect Being, and his glory the noblest end. God is not actively glorified by all men, and therefore he surely did not design it; but he designed to have glory from them, either by them or on them; and so it will be. Happy they who glorify him by their actings, that they may not glorify him by their eternal sufferings.

---

1 Matthew 5:16.
2 Proverbs 16:4.
3 Romans 11:36.

2. It is the end of man as God's work. Man was made fit for glorifying God. "God made man upright";[1] as a well-tuned instrument, or as a house conveniently built, though never inhabited. The very fabric of a man's body, whereby he looks upward, while the beasts look down, is a palpable evidence of this.

3. It is that which man should aim at, the mark to which he should direct all he does, 1 Corinthians 10:31, the text. This is what we should continually have in our eye, the grand design we should be carrying on in the world, "I have set the Lord always before me,"[2] says David.

Secondly, It is man's chief end, that which God chiefly aimed at, the chief end of man as God's work, and that which man should chiefly aim at. God made man for other ends, as to govern, use, and dispose of other creatures in the earth, sea, and air, wisely, soberly, and mercifully.[3] Man was fitted for these ends, and a man may propose them lawfully to himself, seeing God has set them before him; but still these are but subordinate ends to his glory.

There are some ends which men propose to themselves, which are simply unlawful, as to satisfy their revenge, their lust, their covetousness, etc. These are not capable of subordination to the glory of God, who hates robbery for burnt-offering. But there are other ends, which are indeed in themselves lawful, yet become sinful, if they be not set in their due place, that is, subordinate to the glory of God. Now, God's glory is made our chief end, when these three things concur.

1. When whatever end we have in our actions, the glory of God is still one of our ends in acting. We may eat and drink

---

[1] Ecclesiastes 7:29.
[2] Psalm 16:8.
[3] Genesis 1:26.

for the nourishment of our bodies; but this must not jostle out our respect to the glory of God. If the nourishment of our bodies be the only end of our eating and drinking, it is sinful, and out of the due order.

2. It must not only be our end, but it must be our main and principal end, that which we chiefly design. When God's glory is our chief end, all other ends that we propose to ourselves will be down-weighed by this; all other sheaves must bow to that sheaf: as a diligent servant designs to please both the master and his steward, but chiefly the master. But when, on the contrary, a man eats and drinks (for instance) more for the nourishment of his body than for God's glory, it is plain, that God's glory is not the chief end of the man in that action. Hence we read, of some that are "lovers of pleasure more than lovers of God."[1]

3. When it is the ultimate end, the last end, the top and perfection of what we design, beyond which we have no more view, and to which all other ends are made subservient, and as means to that end. Thus we should eat that our bodies may be refreshed; we should desire that our bodies may be refreshed, that we may be the more capable to serve and glorify God in our stations. Thus we are obliged to seek our own salvation, that God may be glorified; and not to seek God's glory only that we may be saved; for that is to make the glory of God a stepping-stone to our own safety.

THIRDLY, I come now to show the extent of this duty. Respect to the glory of God is as salt that must be served up with every dish. The great work of our life is to glorify him; it is the end of our first and of our second creation, "This people have I formed for myself; they shall show forth my praise."[2]

---

1 2 Timothy 3:4.
2 Isaiah 43:21.

We must be for God,[1] and live to him. This must be the end.

1. Of our natural actions, eating, sleeping, walking, etc.[2] we are under a law as to these things. We may not eat and drink as we please, more than pray as we please.[3] All these things must be done in subserviency to the glory of God. These things must be done that we may live, and living may glorify God; and when we can do it without them in heaven, then none of these things shall be done.

2. Of our civil actions, working our work, buying and selling, etc.[4] It was one of the sins of the old world, that they were eating; the word is properly used of beasts eating their food: they had no higher end in it than beasts; and marrying, a thing in itself lawful, but they had no eye to God in it.

3. Of our moral and religious actions.[5] We must pray, hear, etc. for God's glory.

This is such a necessary ingredient in our actions, that none of them are truly good and acceptable to God without it.[6] Do what we will, it cannot be service to God, if we do not make him our end; no more than a servant's working to himself is service to his master. God will never be the rewarder of a work, whereof he is not the end; for if a man should build houses to all the country, if he build not one to me, I owe him nothing. Alas! to what purpose serves a generation of good works all killed by a depraved end?

Though it is a duty frequently to have a formal and express intention of the glory of God in our actings, yet to have it in every action is impossible: neither are we bound to it; for then,

---

1 Hosea 3:3.
2 1 Corinthians 10:31.
3 Zechariah 7:6.
4 Ephesians 6:7; Proverbs 21:4.
5 Zechariah 7:5.
6 Zechariah 7:5.

for that very intention we should be obliged to have another, another for that, and another for that, *in infinitum.* But we should always habitually and interpretatively design the glory of God. And that is done when, (1.) The course of our lives is directed to the glory of God.[1] (2.) When we walk according to the rule of God's Word, taking heed that we swerve not in any thing from it. And, (3.) When God's will is the reason as well as the rule of our actions; when we believe a truth, because God has said it; and do a duty, because God has commanded it. If we do not so, God loses his glory, and we lose our labor.

Fourthly, The reason of the point is, because he is the first principle, therefore he must be the last end. He is the first and the last, the Alpha, and therefore the Omega. God is the fountain of our being; and therefore seeing we *are* of him, we should be *to* him.[2] Man is a mere relative being; God is our Creator, Preserver, and Benefactor. Our being is but a borrowed being from him, as the rays or beams of the sun are borrowed from the sun: therefore I AM is God's name. Whatever perfection we have is from him; hence he is called "the only wise, none good but one, that is God": he gives us the continuance of all these things, and it is on his cost that we live. As when the waters come from the sea unto the earth, and go back again unto it by brooks and rivers; so all we receive and enjoy comes from God, and ought to go back again to him, by being used for his glory. Wherefore to make ourselves our chief end, is to make ourselves a god to ourselves; for a creature to be a center to itself, and that God should be a means to that end, is to blaspheme.[3]

II. I shall speak to the enjoyment of God for ever, wherein

---

1 Psalm 1. ult.
2 Romans 11:36.
3 John 8:50.

man's chief happiness consists, and which he is to seek as his chief good. Here I shall show,

1. The nature of this enjoyment.
2. The order of it.
3. That it is man's chief end in point of happiness.

FIRST, I shall show the nature of this enjoyment. There is a twofold enjoyment of God, imperfect and perfect.

First, There is an imperfect enjoyment of God in this life; which consists in two things.

1. In union with him, or a special saving interest in him, whereby God is their God by covenant. By this union Christ and believers are so joined, that they are one spirit, one mystical body. The whole man, soul and body, is united to him, and, through the Mediator, unto God. This is the foundation of all saving enjoyment of God.

2. In communion with God, which is a participation of the benefits of that saving relation, whereof the soul makes returns to the Lord in the exercise of its graces, particularly of faith and love. This is had in the duties of religion, prayer, meditation, etc. in which the Lord privileges his people with manifestations of his grace, favor, and love, bestows on them the influences of his Spirit, gives them many tokens of his kindness, and fills them with joy and peace in believing.

Secondly, There is a perfect enjoyment of God in heaven, when this world is no more. This consists in,

1. An intimate presence with him in glory "In his presence is fullness of joy, and at his right hand there are pleasures for evermore."[1] God himself shall be with them, and they shall ever be with the Lord, enjoying his glorious presence, brought near to his throne, and standing before him, where he shows his inconceivable glory.

---

1 Psalm 16:11.

2. In seeing him as he is.[1] They shall have a full, a satisfying, and never-ending sight of God, and of all his glorious perfections and excellencies, and they shall be ravished with the view thereof for ever.

3. In a perfect union with him.[2] He will be their God. They were united to God in Christ here by the Spirit and faith, and made partakers of a divine nature, but then only in part; but in heaven they shall perfectly partake of it. There shall be a most close and intimate union between God and them: God shall be in them, and they in God, in the way of a glorious and most perfect union, never to be dissolved.

4. In an immediate, full, free, and comfortable communion with him, infinitely superior to all the communion they ever had with him in this world, and which no mortal can suitably describe.

5. Lastly, In full joy and satisfaction resulting from these things for ever.[3] The presence and enjoyment of God and the Lamb, shall satisfy them with pleasures for evermore. They shall swim for ever in an ocean of joy, and every object they see shall fill them with the most ecstatic joy, which shall be ever fresh and new to them, through all the ages of eternity.[4]

SECONDLY, Let us consider the order of this enjoyment.

1. It is a part of man's chief end, and, in conjunction with glorifying of God, makes it up. And these two are put together, because no man can glorify God, but he that takes God for his chief good and supreme happiness.

2. Glorifying of God is put before the enjoying of him,

---

1 1 John 3:2.
2 Revelation 21:3.
3 Matthew 25:21.
4 The reader may see a more full account of the happiness of the saints in heaven, in the author's book, *Fourfold State*, state 4, head 5.

because the way of duty is the way to the enjoyment of God. Holiness on earth must necessarily go before felicity in heaven.[1] There is an inseparable connection betwixt the two, as between the end and the means; so that no person who does not glorify God here, shall ever enjoy him hereafter. The connection is instituted by God himself, so that the one can never be attained without the other. Let no person, then, who has no regard for the glory and honor of God in this world, dream that he shall be crowned with glory, honor, immortality, and eternal life, in the heavenly mansions. No; the pure in heart, and they who glorify God now, shall alone see God, to their infinite joy in heaven.

THIRDLY, I shall show, that the enjoyment of God is man's chief end in point of happiness, the thing that he should chiefly seek. For this end,

1. Consider what man is. He is, (1.) A creature that desires happiness, and cannot but desire it. The desire of happiness is woven into his nature, and cannot be eradicated. It is as natural for him to desire it as it is to breathe. (2.) He is not self-sufficient: he is conscious to himself that he wants many things, and therefore he is ever seeking something without himself in order to be happy. (3.) Nothing but an infinite good can fully satisfy the desires of an immortal soul: because, whatever good he finds in the creature, he can still desire more, and will continue to desire it; and where it is not to be found, there his happiness is marred. So that man's happiness is neither to be found in himself nor in any creature, or created good.

2. Consider what God is.

First, God is the chief good. Some persons, as angels, etc. and some things, as grace, glory, etc. are good; but God is the chief good, for he is the fountain good, and the water that is

---

1 Hebrews 12:14.

good is always best in the fountain. All other goodness is but second-hand goodness, derived and dependant; but God is original, underived, and independent goodness, the cause and source of whatever is good in heaven and earth. Now, where the more goodness is, there the more it is to be sought. And therefore, seeing God is the chief good, the enjoyment of him is the chief end which man should aim at in seeking.

Secondly, God is all good. (1.) There is nothing in him but what is good; he is entirely without imperfection. (2.) All that is good is in him; so that the soul, finding him commensurate to its desires, needs nothing besides him; and therefore should not, and cannot, fully rest in any person or thing but God, who alone is able to satisfy all its desires, and afford it that happiness which it earnestly pants after.

I shall conclude with a few inferences.

1. O how does reigning sin pervert the spirit of man, turning it quite away from its chief end! How many are there who make themselves their chief end! They are conjured within the circle of self, and out of it they cannot move. Like beasts they grovel on the ground, seeking themselves, and acting for themselves only or chiefly, pursuing the enjoyment of earthly things; but look not to God.[1] Their own advantage is the chief motive and aim they have in their natural, civil, and religious actions, either their own pleasure, profit, or honor and glory. And they never think of, never propose the glory and honor of the infinite Majesty of heaven in any thing they do.

2. This may fill the best with shame and blushing. O how much is God dishonored by our hearts, lips, and lives! O what self-seeking mixes itself with our best actions! How eagerly do we pursue created things, and how faintly the enjoyment of God! How absurd is such conduct! and how dishonorable to

---
1 Philippians 3:19.

a holy God! It is a saying upon the matter, that God is not the chief good, that he is not a suitable portion for the soul, and that the creature is better than God. How should we be ashamed of ourselves on this account, and labor earnestly to make God the chief and ultimate end of all our actions, and the enjoyment of him our chief happiness!

3. Behold the excellency of man above other creatures on earth! He is made for a noble end, to glorify and enjoy God, while other creatures were made for him. How sad is it, that men should thus forget their dignity, and turn slaves to those creatures which were made to serve them! And how deplorable and lamentable is it, that men, in place of making God their ultimate end, and placing their chief happiness in him, should make their belly, their lusts and idols, their God, and place their chief felicity in the gratification of sensual and brutish pleasures; as the drunkard does in his bottle, the unclean person in his whore, the miser in his wealth, and the ambitious man in titles of honor. Alas! our hearts by nature are set on the earth that we tread upon, and our desires reach up to those things that we should make stepping-stones of. Let us earnestly implore divine grace to cure this disorder of our hearts, and give them a bias to more excellent things, and the enjoyment of that which will survive the grave, and not perish with the wrecks of time, and the dissolution of the world.

4. The soul of man is immortal, seeing to enjoy God for ever is its ultimate and supreme happiness. God is immortal, and so must the soul be too, which can never be satisfied but in this never-dying being. The body too must rise again, seeing God is the God and portion of the whole man. Now, God is not the God of the dead, but of the living. Can that thinking and immaterial substance which eagerly desires happiness, and can find it no where but in the immortal God, perish with

the body, and all its thoughts and desires be extinguished in the grave? No; its chief happiness will subsist for ever, and so will the soul too. And both soul and body, which were united to God here, shall continue to be united to him for ever, after the resurrection. Let us then seek to be united to God here, that we may be happy with and in him for ever.

5. When God and the creature come in competition, we must renounce the creature, and cleave to God only.[1] God is the chief good, and to glorify and adhere to him at all times, and in all cases, and amidst all trials, is our great duty, a duty absolutely required of us. If we are reduced to that dilemma, that we must either give up with the creature, or any worldly goods or possessions, or even life itself, or give up with and deny God and his cause, we must give up with and abandon the former, and not prefer them to the glory of God, which we ought always to study as our main end, and account our chief happiness and joy.

6. Here is a rule to try doctrines by, and also practices. Whatever doctrine tends to glorify God, and promote his honor in the world, is certainly from God, and is to be embraced. And whatever practices have that same tendency, they are good, and deserve to be imitated. Whereas any doctrine that tends to dishonor God, to rob him of his glory, and set the crown upon the creature's head, to depreciate the free grace of God, exalt the power of nature and of free-will, in opposition to the efficacious and irresistible grace of God, as the doctrines of the Pelagians, Papists, Arminians, and others do, is not from God. Neither is any doctrine or opinion that robs the Son of God of his essential dignity, supremacy, independency, and equality with the Father, to be received, because it is not of God, who will have all men to honor the Son even as they honor the Father.

---
1 Luke 14:33.

Lastly, Let this then be your main and chief work, to glorify God, and to seek to enjoy him. And hence see the absolute need of Christ, and faith in him; for there is no glorifying of the Father without the Son,[1] and no enjoying of God, but through him. No sacrifice is or can be accepted, unless offered upon this altar; and there is no coming into the chamber of presence, but as introduced by Christ.

---

1 1 John 2:23.

Sermon 2

GOD THE BEST PORTION OF THE CHRISTIAN

By Jonathan Edwards

Whom have I in heaven but thee? and there is none upon earth that I desire besides thee.—PSALM 73:25.

In this psalm, the psalmist (Asaph) relates the great difficulty which existed in his own mind, from the consideration of the wicked. He observes, verses 2 and 3. "As for me, my feet were almost gone; my steps had well nigh slipped. For I was envious at the foolish, when I saw the prosperity of the wicked." In the 4TH and following verses, he informs us, what in the wicked was his temptation. In the first place, he observed, that they were *prosperous*, and all things went well with them. He then observed their *behavior* in their prosperity, and the use which they made of it; and that God, notwithstanding such abuse, *continued* their prosperity. Then he tells us by what means he was helped out of this difficulty, *viz.* by going into the *sanctuary*, verses 16, 17, and proceeds to inform us what considerations they were which helped him, *viz.*—(1.) The consideration of the *miserable end* of wicked men. However they prosper for the present, yet they come to a woeful end at last, verses 18–20.—(2.) The consideration of the *blessed end* of the saints. Although the saints, while they live, may be afflicted, yet they come to a happy end at last, verses 21–24.—(3.) The consideration, that the godly have a much *better portion* than the wicked, even though they have no other portion but God; as in the text and following verse. Though the wicked are in prosperity, and are not in trouble as other men; yet the godly, though in affliction, are in a state infinitely better, because they have God for their portion. They need desire nothing else; he that has God, has all. Thus the psalmist professes the sense and apprehension which he had of things: *Whom have I in heaven but thee? and there is none upon earth that I desire besides thee.*

In the verse immediately preceding, the psalmist takes notice how the saints are happy in God, both when they are in this world, and also when they are taken to another. They are blessed in God in this world, in that he *guides them by his counsel;* and when he takes them out of it, they are still happy, in that then he *receives them to glory*. This probably led him, in the text, to declare that he desired *no other portion*, either in this world or in that to come, either in heaven or upon earth.—Whence we learn, *That it is the spirit of a truly godly man, to prefer God before all other things, either in heaven or on earth.*

I. A godly man prefers God before anything else *in heaven*.

1. He prefers God before any thing else that *actually is* in heaven. Every godly man has his heart in heaven; his affections are mainly set on what is to be had there. Heaven is his chosen country and inheritance. He has respect to heaven, as a traveller, who is in a distant land, has to his own country. The traveller can content himself to be in a strange land for a while, but his own native land is preferred by him to all others. "These all died in faith, not having received the promises, but were persuaded of them, and embraced them, and confessed that

they were strangers and pilgrims on the earth. For they that say such things, declare plainly that they seek a country. And truly if they had been mindful of that country from whence they came out, they might have had opportunity to have returned: but now they desire a better country, that is, a heavenly."[1]— The respect which a godly person has to heaven may be compared to the respect which a child, when he is abroad, has to his father's house. He can be contented abroad for a little while; but the place to which he desires to return, and in which to dwell, is his own home. Heaven is the true saint's Father's house: "In my Father's house are many mansions."[2] "I ascend to my Father and your Father."[3]

Now, the main reason why the godly man has his heart thus to heaven, is because God is there; that is the palace of the Most High. It is the place where God is gloriously present, where his love is gloriously manifested, where the godly may be with him, see him as he is, and love, serve, praise, and enjoy him perfectly. If God and Christ were not in heaven, he would not be so earnest in seeking it, nor would he take so much pains in a laborious travel through this wilderness, nor would the consideration that he is going to heaven when he dies, be such a comfort to him under toils and afflictions. The martyrs would not undergo cruel sufferings, from their persecutors, with a cheerful prospect of going to heaven, did they not expect to be with Christ, and to enjoy God there. They would not with that cheerfulness forsake all their earthly possessions, and all their earthly friends, as many thousands of them have done, and wander about in poverty and banishment, being destitute, afflicted, tormented, in hopes of exchanging their

---

1 Hebrews 11:13–16.
2 John 14:2.
3 John 20:17.

earthly for a heavenly inheritance, were it not that they hope to be with their glorious Redeemer and heavenly Father.—The believer's heart is in heaven, because his treasure is there.

2. *A godly man prefers God before any thing else that might be* in heaven. Not only is there nothing *actually* in heaven, which is in his esteem equal to God; but neither is there any of which he can conceive as *possible to be there*, which by him is esteemed and desired equally with God. Some suppose quite different enjoyments to be in heaven, from those which the Scriptures teach us. The Mahometans, for instance, suppose that in heaven are to be enjoyed all manner of sensual delights and pleasures. Many things which Mahomet has feigned are to the lusts and carnal appetites of men the most agreeable that he could devise, and with them he flatters his followers.—But the true saint could not contrive one more agreeable to his inclination and desires, than such as is revealed in the Word of God; a heaven of enjoying the glorious God, and the Lord Jesus Christ. There he shall have all sin taken away, and shall be perfectly conformed to God, and shall spend an eternity in exalted exercises of love to him, and in the enjoyment of his love. If God were not to be enjoyed in heaven, but only vast wealth, immense treasures of silver, and gold, great honor of such kind as men obtain in this world, and a fullness of the greatest sensual delights and pleasures; all these things would not make up for the want of God and Christ, and the enjoyment of them there. If it were empty of God, it would indeed be an empty melancholy place.—The godly have been made sensible, as to all creature-enjoyments, that they cannot satisfy the soul; and therefore nothing will content them but God. Offer a saint what you will, if you deny him God, he will esteem himself miserable. God is the center of his desires; and as long as you keep his soul from its proper center, it will not be at rest.

II. It is the temper of a godly man to prefer God before all other things *on the earth.*

1. The saint prefers that enjoyment of God, for which he *hopes* hereafter, to any thing in this world. He looks not so much at the things which are seen and temporal, as at those which are unseen and eternal.[1] It is but a little of God that the saint enjoys in this world; he has but a little acquaintance with God, and enjoys but a little of the manifestations of the divine glory and love. But God has promised to give him himself hereafter in a full enjoyment. And these promises are more precious to the saint, than the most precious earthly jewels. The gospel contains greater treasures, in his esteem, than the cabinets of princes, or the mines of the Indies.

2. The saint prefers what of God may be *obtained* in this life before all things in the world. There is a great difference in the present spiritual attainments of the saints. Some attain to much greater acquaintance and communion with God, and conformity to him, than others. But the highest attainments are very small in comparison with what is future. The saints are capable of making progress in spiritual attainments, and they earnestly desire such further attainments. Not contented with those degrees to which they have already attained, they hunger and thirst after righteousness, and, as new-born babes, desire the sincere milk of the Word, that they may grow thereby. It is their desire, to know more of God, to have more of his image, and to be enabled more to imitate God and Christ in their walk and conversation. "One thing have I desired of the Lord, that will I seek after, that I may dwell in the house of the Lord all the days of my life, to behold the beauty of the Lord, and to inquire in his temple."[2] "As the hart panteth after the

---

1 1 Corinthians 4:18.
2 Psalm 27:4.

water-brooks, so panteth my soul after thee, O God. My soul thirsteth for God, for the living God: when shall I come and appear before God?"[1] "O God, thou art my God, early will I seek thee: my soul thirsteth for thee, my flesh longeth for thee in a dry and thirsty land, where no water is; to see thy power and thy glory, so as I have seen thee in the sanctuary."[2] "My soul waiteth for the Lord, more than they that watch for the morning; I say, more than they that watch for the morning."[3]

Though every saint has not this longing desire after God to the same degree that the psalmist had, yet they are all of the same spirit; they earnestly desire to have more of his presence in their hearts. That this is the temper of the godly in general, and not of some particular saints only, appears from Isaiah 26:8, 9; where not any particular saint, but the church in general speaks thus: "Yea, in the way of thy judgments, O Lord, have we waited for thee; the desire of our soul is to thy name, and to the remembrance of thee. With my soul have I desired thee in the night, and with my spirit within me will I seek thee early."[4]

The saints are not always in the lively exercise of grace: but such a spirit they have, and sometimes they have the sensible exercise of it. They desire God and divine attainments, more than all earthly things; and seek to be rich in grace, more than they do to get earthly riches. They desire the honor which is of God, more than that which is of men,[5] and communion with him, more than any earthly pleasures. They are of the same spirit which the apostle expresses, "Yea, doubtless, and I count all things but loss, for the excellency of the knowledge

1 Psalm 42:1, 2.
2 Psalm 63:1, 2.
3 Psalm 130:6; Psalm 84:1, 2, 3.
4 See also Song of Solomon 3:1, 2; 5:6, 8.
5 John 5:44.

of Christ Jesus, my Lord, and do count them but dung that I may win Christ."¹

3. The saint prefers *what he has already of God* before any thing in this world. That which was infused into his heart at his conversion, is more precious to him than any thing which the world can afford. The views which are sometimes given him of the beauty and excellency of God, are more precious to him than all the treasures of the wicked. The relation of a child in which he stands to God, the union which there is between his soul and Jesus Christ, he values more than the greatest earthly dignity. That image of God which is instamped on his soul, he values more than any earthly ornaments. It is, in his esteem, better to be adorned with the graces of God's Holy Spirit, than to be made to shine in jewels of gold, and the most costly pearls, or to be admired for the greatest external beauty. He values the robe of Christ's righteousness, which he has on his soul, more than the robes of princes. The spiritual pleasures and delights which he sometimes has in God, he prefers far before all the pleasures of sin. "A day in thy courts is better than a thousand: I had rather be a doorkeeper in the house of God, than to dwell in the tents of wickedness."²

A saint thus prefers God before all other things in this world.—1. As he prefers God before any thing else that he *possesses* in the world. Whatever temporal enjoyments he has, he prefers God to them all. "The Lord is the portion of mine inheritance, and of my cup: thou maintainest my lot. The lines are fallen to me in pleasant places; yea, I have a goodly heritage."³ If he be rich, he chiefly sets his heart on his heavenly riches. He prefers God before any earthly friend, and the

---

1 Philippians 3:8.
2 Psalm 84:10.
3 Psalm 16:5, 6.

divine favor before any respect shown him by his fellow-creatures. Although inadvertently these have room in his heart, and too much room; yet he reserves the throne for God; "If man come to me, and hate not his father and mother, and wife, and children, and brethren, and sisters, yea, and his own life also, he cannot be my disciple."[1]

2. He prefers God before any earthly enjoyment of which he *has a prospect*. The children of men commonly set their hearts more on some earthly happiness for which they *hope*, and after which they are seeking, than on what they *have* in present possession. But a godly man prefers God to any thing which he has in prospect in this world. He may, indeed, through the prevalence of corruption, be for a season carried away with some enjoyment; however, he will again come to himself; this is not the temper of the man; he is of another spirit.

3. It is the spirit of a godly man to prefer God to any earthly enjoyments of which he *can conceive.* He not only prefers him to any thing which he now possesses; but he sees nothing by any of his fellow-creatures, so estimable. Could he have as much worldly prosperity as he would, could he have earthly things just to his mind, and agreeable to his inclination; he values the portion which he has in God, incomparably more. He prefers Christ to earthly kingdoms.

APPLICATION

1. Hence we may learn that whatever changes a godly man passes through, he is happy; because God, who is unchangeable, is his chosen portion. Though he meet with temporal losses, and be deprived of many, yea, of all his temporal enjoyments; yet God, whom he prefers before all, still remains, and

---
1 Luke 14:26.

cannot be lost. While he stays in this changeable, troublesome world, he is happy; because his chosen portion, on which he builds as his main foundation for happiness, is above the world, and above all changes. And when he goes into another world, still he is happy, because that portion yet remains. Whatever he be deprived of, he cannot be deprived of his chief portion; his inheritance remains sure to him.—Could worldly-minded men find out a way to secure to themselves those earthly enjoyments on which they mainly set their hearts, so that they could not be lost nor impaired while they live, how great would they account the privilege, though other things which they esteem in a less degree, were liable to the same uncertainty as they now are! Whereas now, those earthly enjoyments, on which men chiefly set their hearts, are often most fading. But how great is the happiness of those who have chosen the Fountain of all good, who prefer him before all things in heaven or on earth, and who can never be deprived of him to all eternity!

2. Let all by these things examine and try themselves, whether they be saints or not. As this which has been exhibited is the spirit of the saints, so it is peculiar to them: none can use the language of the text, and say, *Whom have I in heaven but thee? there is none upon earth that I desire besides thee,* but the saints. A man's choice is that which determines his state. He that chooses God for his portion, and prefers him to all other things, is a godly man, for *he* chooses and worships him as God. To respect him as God, is to respect him above all other things; and if any man respect him as *his* God, *his God he is;* there is an union and covenant relation between that man and the true God.—Every man is as his God is. If you would know what a man is, whether he be a godly man or not, you must inquire what his God is. If the true God be he to whom he has a supreme respect, whom he regards above

all; he is doubtless a servant of the true God. But if the man have something else to which he pays a greater respect than to Jehovah, he is not a godly man.

Inquire, therefore, how it is with you—whether you prefer God before all other things. It may sometimes be a difficulty for persons to determine this to their satisfaction; the ungodly may be deluded with false affections; the godly in dull frames may be at a loss about it. Therefore you may try yourselves, as to this matter, several ways; if you cannot speak fully to one thing, yet you may perhaps to others.

1. What is it which *chiefly* makes you desire to go to heaven when you die? Indeed some have no great desire to go to heaven. They do not care to go to hell; but if they could be safe from that, they would not much concern themselves about heaven. If it be not so with you, but you find that you have a desire after heaven, then inquire what it is for. Is the main reason, that you may be with God, have communion with him, and be conformed to him? that you may see God, and enjoy him there? Is this the consideration which keeps your hearts, and your desires, and your expectations towards heaven?

2. If you could avoid death, and might have your free choice, would you choose to live *always* in this world without God, rather than in his time to leave the world, in order to be with him? If you might live here in earthly prosperity to all eternity, but destitute of the presence of God and communion with him—having no spiritual intercourse between him and your souls, God and you being strangers to each other for ever—would you choose this rather than to leave the world, in order to dwell in heaven, as the children of God, there to enjoy the glorious privileges of children, in a holy and perfect love to God, and enjoyment of him to all eternity?

3. Do you prefer Christ to all others as the *way* to heaven?

He who truly chooses God, prefers him in each person of the Trinity, Father, Son, and Holy Ghost: the Father, as his Father; the Son as his Saviour; the Holy Ghost, as his Sanctifier. Inquire, therefore, not only whether you choose the enjoyment of God in heaven as your highest portion and happiness, but also whether you choose Jesus Christ before all others, as your way to heaven; and that in a sense of the excellency of Christ, and of the way of salvation by him, as being that which is to the glory of Christ, and of sovereign grace. Is the way of free grace, by the blood and righteousness of the blessed and glorious Redeemer, the most excellent way to life in your esteem? Does it add a value to the heavenly inheritance, that it is conferred in this way? Is this far better to you than to be saved by your own righteousness, by any of your own performances, or by any other mediator?

4. If you might go to heaven in what course you please, would you prefer to all others the way of a *strict walk* with God? They who prefer God as has been represented, choose him, not only in the end, but in the way. They had rather be with God than with any other, not only when they come to the end of their journey; but also while they are in their pilgrimage. They choose the way of walking with God, though it be a way of labor, and care, and self-denial, rather than a way of sin, though it be a way of sloth, and of gratifying their lusts.

5. Were you to spend your eternity in this world, would you choose rather to live in mean and low circumstances with the gracious presence of God, than to live for ever in earthly prosperity without him? Would you rather spend it in holy living, and serving and walking with God, and in the enjoyment of the privileges of his children? God often manifesting himself to you as your Father, discovering to you his glory, and manifesting his love, lifting the light of his countenance upon you!

Would you rather choose these things, though in poverty, than to abound in worldly things, and to live in ease and prosperity, at the same time being an alien from the commonwealth of Israel? Could you be content to stand in no child-like relation to God, enjoying no gracious intercourse with him, having no right to be acknowledged by him as his children? Or would such a life as this, though in ever so great earthly prosperity, be esteemed by you a miserable life?

If, after all, there remain with you doubts, and a difficulty to determine concerning yourselves whether you do truly and sincerely prefer God to all other things, I would mention two things which are the surest ways to be determined in this matter, and which seem to be the best grounds of satisfaction in it.

1. The feeling of some particular, strong, and lively *exercise* of such a spirit. A person may have such a spirit as is spoken of in the doctrine, and may have the exercise of it in a low degree, and yet remain in doubt whether he have it or not, and be unable to come to a satisfying determination. But God is pleased sometimes to give such discoveries of his glory, and of the excellency of Christ, as do so draw forth the heart, that they know beyond all doubt, that they feel such a spirit as Paul spoke of, when he said, "he counted all things but loss for the excellency of Christ Jesus his Lord"; and they can boldly say, as in the text, "Whom have I in heaven but thee? and there is none upon earth that I desire besides thee." At such times the people of God do not need any help of ministers to satisfy them whether they have the true love of God; they plainly see and feel it; and the Spirit of God then witnesses with their spirits, that they are the children of God.—Therefore, if you would be satisfied upon this point, earnestly seek such attainments; seek that you may have such clear and lively exercises of this spirit. To this end, you must labor to grow in grace. Though you

have had such experiences in times past, and they satisfied you then, yet you may again doubt. You should therefore seek that you may have them more frequently; and the way to that is, earnestly to press forward, that you may have more acquaintance with God, and have the principles of grace strengthened. This is the way to have the exercises of grace stronger, more lively, and more frequent, and so to be satisfied that you have a spirit of supreme love to God.

2. The other way is, To inquire whether you prefer God to all other things in *practice, i.e.* when you have occasion to manifest by your practice which you prefer—when you must either cleave to one or the other, and must either forsake other things, or forsake God—whether then it be your manner practically to prefer God to all other things whatever, even to those earthly things to which your hearts are most wedded. Are your lives those of adherence to God, and of serving him in this manner?

He who sincerely prefers God to all other things in his heart, will do it in his practice. For when God and all other things come to stand in competition, that is the proper trial what a man chooses; and the manner of acting in such cases must certainly determine what the choice is in all free agents, or those who act on choice. Therefore there is no sign of sincerity so much insisted on in the Bible as this, that we deny ourselves, sell all, forsake the world, take up the cross, and follow Christ whithersoever he goes.—Therefore, so run, not as uncertainly; so fight, not as those that beat the air; but keep under your bodies, and bring them into subjection. Act not as though you counted yourselves to have apprehended; but this one thing do, "forgetting those things which are behind, and reaching forth unto those things which are before, press toward the mark, for the prize of the high calling of God in Christ Jesus."[1]

1 Philippians 3:13, 14.

"And besides this, giving diligence, add to your faith, virtue; and to virtue, knowledge; and to knowledge, temperance; and to temperance, patience; and to patience, godliness; and to godliness, brotherly kindness; and to brotherly kindness, charity. For if these things be in you, and abound, they make you that ye shall neither be barren nor unfruitful in the knowledge of our Lord Jesus Christ."[1]

Dated April, 1736.

---

1 2 Peter 1:5–8.

Sermon 3

The Attributes of God As Our Portion

By George Swinnock

First, God is a satisfying portion. The things of this world may surfeit a man, but they can never satisfy him. Most men have too much, but no man has enough; as ships, they have that burden which sinks them when they have room to hold more. "He that loveth silver is not satisfied with silver, nor he that loveth gold with increase."[1] Worldlings are like the Parthians, the more they drink, the more they thirst. As the melancholy chemist, they work eagerly to find the philosopher's stone, rest and happiness in it, though they have experience of its vanity, and it has already brought them to beggary. The world cannot satisfy the senses, much less the soul: the eye is not satisfied with seeing, nor the ear with hearing.

As the apes in the story, finding a glow-worm in a frosty night, took it for a spark of fire, gathered some sticks, and leaped on it, expecting to be warmed by it, but all in vain: so men think to find warmth and satisfaction in creatures; but they are as the clothes to David, when stricken in years, though covered with them, not able to give any heat. Where shall contentment be found, and where is the place of satisfaction?

1 Ecclesiastes 5:10.

The depth says, It is not in me; and the earth says, It is not in me: nay, heaven itself, were God out of it, would say, It is not in me.

Reader, you long for the things of this world, and think, could you have but a table full of such dishes, you should feed heartily, and fill yourself. But do you not know they are like the meat which sick men cry so much for, that, when brought to them, they can taste of possibly, but not at all fill themselves with. The pond of the creature has so much mud at the bottom, that none can have a full draught. The sun and moon seem bigger at first rising than when they come to be over our heads. All outward things are great in expectation, but nothing in fruition. The world promises as much, and performs as little, as the tomb of Semiramis. When she had built a stately tomb, she caused this inscription to be engraven on it: Whatsoever king shall succeed here, and want money, let him open this tomb, and he shall have enough to serve his turn; which Darius afterwards, wanting money, opened, and, instead of riches, found this sharp reproof: Unless you had been extremely covetous and greedy of filthy lucre, you would not have opened the grave of the dead to seek for money. Thus many run to the world with high hopes, and return with nothing but blanks. Hence it is that worldlings are said to feed on lies, and to suck wind from this strumpet's breasts, both which are far from filling.[1]

Reader, since the controversy is so great amongst men, whether rest does not grow on the furrows of the field, and happiness in the mines of gold; whether creatures wisely distilled may not have happiness drawn out of them, let us hear the judgment of one that enjoyed the world at will, and had prudence enough to extract the quintessence of it; who was

1 Hosea 10:13 and 12:1.

thoroughly furnished with all variety of requisites for such an undertaking, who did set himself curiously to anatomise the body of the creation. And what is the result? "Vanity of vanities; all is vanity," says the preacher. Mark,

1. Vanity in the abstract; not *vain*, but *vanity*.

2. Plurality, Vanity *of vanities;* excessive vanity, all over vanity, nothing but vanity.

3. Universality, *All* is vanity: everything severally, all things collectively. Riches are vanity,[1] honors are vanity; pleasures are vanity; knowledge is vanity; all is vanity.

4. The verity of all this, *says the preacher;* one that speaks not by guess or hearsay, but by experience, who had tried the utmost that the creature could do, and found it to come far short of satisfying man's desire; one that spoke not only his own opinion, but by divine inspiration; yet the total of the account which he gives in, after he had reckoned up all the creatures, is nothing but ciphers; "Vanity of vanities, all is vanity," says the preacher.

Men that are in the valley think, if they were at the top of such a hill, they should touch the heavens. Men that are in the bottom of poverty, or disgrace, or pain, think, if they could get up to such a mountain, such a measure of riches, and honors, and delights, they could reach happiness. Now Solomon had got to the top of this hill, and seeing so many scrambling and laboring so hard, nay, riding on one another's necks, and pressing one another to death to get foremost, does seem thus to bespeak them: Sirs, you are all deceived in your expectations; I see the pains you take to get up to this place, thinking, that when you come hither, you shall touch the heavens, and reach happiness; but I am before you at the top of the hill—I have treasures, and honors, and pleasures in variety and

---

1 Ecclesiastes 2.

abundance¹—and I find the hill full of quagmires instead of delights, and so far from giving me satisfaction, that it causes much vexation; therefore be advised to spare your pains, and spend your strength for that which will turn to more profit; for, believe it, you do but work at the labor in vain. "Vanity of vanities, all is vanity," says the preacher.

We have weighed the world in the balance, and found it lighter than vanity; let us see what weight God has. David will tell us, though the vessel of the creature be frozen, that no satisfaction can be drawn thence, yet this fountain runs freely to the full content of all true Christians: "The Lord is the portion of my cup, and inheritance; thou maintainest my lot."² The former expression, is an allusion to the custom of dividing their drink at banquets, the latter to the division of Canaan by lot and line,³ according as the lot fell, was every one's part. Now David's part and lot fell, it seems, like the Levites under the law, on God, but is he pleased in his portion, and can he take any delight in his estate? "The lines are fallen to me in a pleasant place, yea, I have a goodly heritage."⁴ As if he had said, No lot ever fell in a better land; my portion happens in the best place that is possible; my knowledge of thee and propriety in thee affords full content and felicity to me. I have enough, and crave no more; I have all, and can have no more. Though creatures bring in an *ignoramus* to that inquiry concerning satisfaction, yet the all-sufficient God does not.

If it were possible for one man to be crowned with the royal diadem and dominion of the whole world, and to enjoy all the treasures, and honors, and pleasures that all the kingdoms on

---

1 Ecclesiastes 2:12, 13.
2 Psalm 16:5.
3 Psalm 78:55.
4 Psalm 16:5, 6.

earth can yield, if his senses and understanding were enlarged to the utmost of created capacities, to taste and take in whatsoever comfort and delight the universe can give; if he had the society of glorious angels and glorified saints thrown into the bargain, and might enjoy all this the whole length of the world's duration, yet without God would this man in the midst of all this be unsatisfied; these things, like dew, might wet the branches, please the flesh, but would leave the root dry, the spirit discontented. Once admit the man to the sight of God, and let God but possess his heart, and then, and not before, his infinite desires expire in the bosom of his Maker. Now the weary dove is at rest, and the vessel tossed up and down on the waters is quiet in its haven. There is in the heart of man such a drought, without this river of paradise, that all the waters in the world, though every drop were an ocean, cannot quench it. Oh what dry chips are all creatures to a hungry immortal soul! Lord, says Augustine, thou have made our heart for thee, and it will never rest till it come to thee; and when I shall wholly cleave to thee, then my life will be lively.[1]

There are two special faculties in man's soul, which must be answered with suitable and adequate objects, or the heart, like the sea, cannot rest. The understanding must be satisfied with truth, and the will with good. For the filling of these two faculties men are as busy as bees, flying over the field of the world, and trying every flower for sweetness, but after all their toil and labor, house themselves, like wasps, in curious combs without any honey. The understanding must be suited with the highest truth; but the world is a lie,[2] and the things thereof are called lying vanities; they are not what they seem to be,[3]

---

1 Augustine's Confessions.
2 Psalm 62.
3 Jonah 2:8.

and hence are unable to satisfy the mind; but God is *æterna veritas, et vera æternitas*, eternal truth, and true eternity. All truth is originally in him; his nature is the idea of truth, and his will the standard of truth; and it is eternal life and utmost satisfaction to know him, because by it the understanding is perfected; for the soul in God will see all truth, and that not only clearly—I speak of the other world, where the Christian's happiness shall be completed—face to face, but also fully. Aristotle, though a heathen, thought happiness to consist in the knowledge of the chiefest good. If Archimedes, when he found out the resolution of one question in the mathematics was so ravished that he ran up and down crying, I have found it, I have found it; how will the Christian be transported when he shall know all that is knowable, and all shadows of ignorance vanish as the darkness before the rising sun. The will also must be suited with good, and according to the degree of goodness in the object, such is the degree of satisfaction to the faculty. Now the things of this life, though good in themselves, yet are vain and evil by reason of the sin of man,[1] and likewise are at best but bodily, limited, and fading good things, and therefore incapable of filling this faculty. As truth in the utmost latitude is the object of the understanding, so good in the universality of it is the object of the will. Further, that good which satisfies must be *optimum*, the best, or it will never *sistere appetitum,* the soul will otherwise be still longing; and *maximum*, the most perfect, or it will never *implere appetitum*, fill it. But God is such a good, he is essentially, universally, unchangeably, and infinitely good, and therefore satisfies. "When I awake I shall be satisfied with thy likeness."[2] When my body has slept in the bed of the grave till the morning of the resurrection,

---

1 Romans 8:20.
2 Psalm 17:15.

and the sound of the last trump shall awaken me, oh the sweet satisfaction and ravishing delight which my soul shall enjoy in being full of thy likeness and thy love! Nay, in the meantime, before the happiness of a saint appear to his view in a full body, it does, like the rising sun, with its forerunning rays, cast such a lightsome, gladsome brightness upon the believer, that he is filled with joy at present, and would not part with his hopes of it for the whole world in hand. "They shall be abundantly satisfied with the fatness of thy house, (while on this side heaven;) and thou shalt make them drink of the rivers of thy pleasures."[1] Though the wedding dinner be deferred till the wedding-day, yet beforehand the Christian meets with many a running banquet. He has not only pleasures, "fatness of thy house," but also plenty of it here below: "They shall be abundantly satisfied."

The world is like sharp sauce, which does not fill, but provoke the stomach to call for more. The voice of those guests whom it makes most welcome, is like the daughters of the horseleech, Give, give; but the infinite God, like solid food, satisfies the soul fully, ("in my Father's house is bread enough") and causes it to cry out, I have enough.

SECONDLY, GOD IS A SANCTIFYING, ENNOBLING PORTION. The world cannot advance the soul in the least. Things of the world are fitly compared to shadows, for be thy shadow never so long, thy body is not the longer for it; so be thy estate never so great, thy soul is not the better for it. A great letter makes no more to the signification of a word than the smallest. Men in high places are the same men, no real worth being thereby added to them, that they are in low ones.

Nay, it is too too visible that men are the worse for their earthly portions. If some had not been so wealthy, they had

---

1 Psalm 36:8.

not been so wicked. Most of the world's favorites, like aguish stomachs, are fuller of appetite than digestion; they eat more than they can concoct, and thereby cause diseases; nay, by feeding on this trash of earth, their stomachs are taken off from substantial food, the bread of heaven. The soldiers of Hannibal were effeminated, and made unfit for service, by their pleasures at Capua. Damps arising out of the earth have stifled many a soul. Aristotle tells us of a sea wherein, by the hollowness of the earth under it, or some whirling property, ships used to be cast away in the midst of a calm.[1] Many perish in their greatest prosperity; and are so busy about babies and rattles, that they have no leisure to be saved.[2]

That which elevates and ennoble the soul of man must be more excellent than the soul. Silver is embased by mixing it with lead, but ennobled by gold, because the former is inferior to it, but the latter excels it. The world and all things in it are infinitely inferior to the soul of man; and therefore it is debased by mingling with them; but God is infinitely superior, and so advances it by joining with it. That coin which is the most excellent metal defiles our hands, and is apt to defile our hearts; but the divine nature elevates and purifies the spirit.

The goodliest portions of this life are like the cities which Solomon gave to Hiram. "And Hiram came from Tyre to see the cities which Solomon had given him; and they pleased him not. And he said, What cities are these which thou have given me, my brother? And he called them the land of Cabul (that is, displeasing or dirty) unto this day."[3] The pleasantest portion here lies in the land of Cabul; it is displeasing and dirty; it does both dissatisfy and defile, when the heavenly portion does, like

---

1 Aristotle's Problemata, sect. 23.
2 Luke 14:18.
3 1 Kings 9:12, 13.

honey, both delight and cleanse, both please and purify.

Outward things, like common stones to a ring, add nothing at all to the worth of a soul; but this sparkling diamond, this pearl of price, the infinite God, makes the gold ring of the soul to be of unspeakable value. "The heart of the wicked is little worth."[1] His house is worth somewhat, but his heart is worth nothing, because it is a ditch full only of dirt; his earthly portion has possession of it; but the heart of a godly man is worth millions, because it is the cabinet where this inestimable jewel is laid up. "The righteous is more excellent than his neighbor,"[2] because he partakes of the divine nature. God, like gold, enriches whatsoever he is joined to; hence it is that things which excel in Scripture are usually said to be things of God; as the garden of God,[3] the hill of God,[4] the mountains of God,[5] a city of God,[6] the cedars of God[7]—that is, the most excellent garden, hill, mountain, city, and cedars. God is the perfection of your soul; and therefore would, if your portion, advance it to purpose. Oh what a height of honor and happiness would you arrive at if this God were yours! Now like a worm thou crawls on, and dwells in the earth, the meanest and basest of all the elements, that which brutes trample under their feet; but then like an eagle you would mount up to heaven, contemning these toys, and leaving those babies for children, and, as an angel, always stand in the presence of, and enjoy unspeakable pleasure in him who is your portion. Your life at present is low, little differing from the life of a beast,

---

1 Proverbs 10:20.
2 Proverbs 12:26.
3 Ezekiel 28:13.
4 Psalm 68:15.
5 Psalm 36:6.
6 John 3:3.
7 Psalm 80:10.

consisting chiefly in making provision for—that which should be your slave—the flesh; but your life then would be high and noble, much resembling the lives of those honorable courtiers, whose continual practice is to adore and admire the blessed and only potentate.

Do you not find by experience that earthly things obstruct holiness, and thereby hinder your soul's happiness? Alas! the best of them are but like the wings of a butterfly, which, though curiously painted, foul the fingers; but if your heart had but once closed with God as your portion, it would be every day more pure, and nearer to perfection. You have, it may be, gold and silver; why, the Midianites' camels had chains of gold, and were they ever the better?[1] Many brutes have had silver bells, but their natures brutish still; but oh the excellency which God would add to your soul by bestowing on it his own likeness and love!

THIRDLY, GOD IS A UNIVERSAL PORTION.[2] God has in himself eminently and infinitely all good things; and creatures are bounded in their beings, and therefore in the comfort which they yield. Health answers sickness, but it does not answer poverty. Honor is a help against disgrace, but not against pain. Money is the most universal medicine, and therefore is said to answer all things; but as great a monarch as it is, it can neither command ease in sickness, nor honors in disgrace, much less quiet a wounded spirit. At best, creatures are but particular beings, and so but particular blessings. Now man, being a compound of many wants and weaknesses, can never be happy till he find a salve for every sore, and a remedy which bears proportion as well to the number as nature of his maladies. Ahab, though in his ivory palace, upon his throne

---
1 Judges 8:26.
2 Operari sequitur esse.

of glory, attended with his noble lords, and swaying a large scepter, was miserable because the heavens were brass. Haman, though he had the favor of the prince, the adoration of the people, the sway of a hundred and twenty-seven provinces, yet is discontented because he wanted Mordecai's knee. If the world's darlings enjoy many good things, yet they, as Christ told the young man, always lack one thing, which makes them at a loss.

But God is all good things, and every good thing. He is self-sufficient, alone-sufficient, and all-sufficient. Nothing is wanting in him, either for the soul's protection from all evil, or perfection with all good. Reader, if God were your portion, you should find in him whatsoever your heart could desire, and whatsoever could tend to your happiness. Are you ambitious? He is a crown of glory, and a royal diadem. Are you covetous? He is unsearchable riches, yea, durable riches and righteousness. Are you voluptuous? He is rivers of pleasures and fullness of joy. Are you hungry? He is a feast of wine on the lees, of fat things full of marrow. Are you weary? He is rest, a shadow from the heat, and a shelter from the storm. Are you weak? In the Lord Jehovah is everlasting strength. Are you in doubts? He is marvellous in counsel. Are you in darkness? He is the Sun of righteousness, an eternal light. Are you sick? He is the God of your health. Are you sorrowful? He is the God of all consolations. Are you dying? He is the fountain and Lord of life. Are you in any distress? His name is a strong tower; there you may run and find safety. He is παν φάρμακον, a universal medicine against all sorts of miseries. Whatsoever thy calamity is, he could remove it; whatsoever thy necessity, he could relieve it. He is silver, gold, honor, delight, food, raiment, house, land, peace, wisdom, power, beauty, father, mother, wife, husband, mercy, love, grace, glory, and infinitely more than all these.

God and all his creatures are no more than God without any of his creatures. As the Jews say of manna, that it had all sorts of delicate tastes in it; it is most true of God, he has all sorts of delights in him.[1] This tree of life bears twelve manner of fruits every month.[2] There is in it both variety and plenty of comforts. The former prevents our loathing, the latter our lacking.

One being desirous to see the famous city of Athens, was told, *Viso Solone vidisti omnia*, See but Solon; and in him you may see all the rarities and excellencies in it. Reader, would you see all the wealth and worth of sea and land? Would you be upon the pinnacle of the temple, as Christ was, and behold, and have the offer of all the kingdoms of the world and the glory of them? Nay, would you view heaven's glorious city, the royal palace of the great King, the costly curious workmanship about it, and the unheard-of rarities and delights in that court, which infinite embroidered wisdom contrived, boundless power and love erected, and infinite bounty enriched? You may both see and enjoy all this in God. See but God, and you see all; enjoy but God, and you enjoy all in him.

As a merchant in London may trade for and fetch in the horses of Barbary, the Canary sacks, the French wines, the Spanish sweetmeats, the oils of Candia, the spices of Egypt, the artificial wares of Alexandria, the silks of Persia, the embroideries of Turkey, the golden wedges of India, the emeralds of Scythia, the topazes of Ethiopia, and the diamonds of Bisnager, so might you, were but this God your portion, fetch in the finest bread to feed you, the choicest wine to comfort you, oil to cheer you, joy to refresh you, raiment to clothe you, the jewels of grace to beautify you, and the crown of glory to make you

---

1 Quid quæris extra illum? quid desideras præter illum? quid placet cum illo?—*Bernardi Serm. de Misce. Com.*
2 Revelation 22:2.

blessed, nay, all the wealth of this and the other world. If all the riches in the covenant of grace, if all the good things which Christ purchased with his precious blood, nay, if as much good as is in an infinite God can make you happy, you should have it. If David were thought worth ten thousand Israelites, how much is the God of Israel worth?

This one God would fill up your soul in its utmost capacity. It is such an end that when you attain you could go no farther, should desire no more, but quietly rest for ever. The necessity of the creatures' number speaks the meanness of their value; but the universality of good in this one God proclaims his infinite worth. As there are all parts of speech in that one verse,

"Væ tibi ridenti, quia mox post gaudia flebis"

so there are all perfections in this one God. What a portion is this friend!

FOURTHLY, GOD IS AN ETERNAL PORTION. The pleasures of sin are but for a season, a little inch of time, a τὸ νῦν, a season is a very short space,[1] but the portion of a saint is for ever. "God is the strength of my heart, and my portion for ever." The greatest estate here below is a flood soon up and soon down; but if God say once to thy soul, as to Aaron's, "I am thine inheritance,"[2] neither men nor devils can cozen thee of it. "The Lord knoweth the days of the upright; and their inheritance shall be for ever."[3]

The prodigal wasted his portion, and so came to poverty. The glutton swallows down his portion, burying it in his belly. The drunkard vomits up his portion. The ambitious person

---

1 Hebrews 11.
2 Numbers 18:20.
3 Psalm 37:18.

often turns his portion into smoke, and it vanishes in the air. Those whose portion continues longest will be turned out of possession, when death once comes with a writ from heaven to seal a lease of ejectment; for all these portions are dying gourds, deceitful brooks, and flying shadows. But ah, how contrary hereunto is the portion of a believer! God is an eternal portion. If he were once your portion, he would be for ever your portion. When your estate, and children, and wife, and honors, and all earthly things should be taken from you, he is the good part which shall never be taken from you.[1] Your friends may use you as a suit of apparel, which, when they have worn threadbare, they throw off, and call for new. Your relations may serve you as women their flowers, who stick them in their bosoms when fresh and flourishing; but, when dying and withered, they throw them to the dunghill. Your riches, and honors, and pleasures, and wife, and children, may stand on the shore and see you launching into the ocean of eternity, but will not step one foot into the water after you; you may sink or swim for them. Only this God is your portion, will never leave thee nor forsake thee.[2] Oh how happy would you be in having such a friend! Your portion would be tied to you in this life, as Dionysius thought his kingdom was to him, with chains of adamant; there would be no severing it from you. The world could not; you should live above the world while you walk about it, and behave yourself in it, not as its champion, but conqueror. "He that is born of God, overcomes the world."[3] Satan should not part you and your portion. Your God has him in his chain; and though, like a mastiff without teeth, he may bark, yet he can never bite or hurt his children. "I have

---

[1] Luke 10:42.
[2] Hebrews 13:5.
[3] 1 John 5:4.

written unto you, young men, because ye have overcome the wicked one."¹ Nay, it should not be in your own power to sell away your portion. You would be a joint-heir with Christ, and co-heirs cannot sell, except both join; and Christ knows the worth of this inheritance too well to part with it for all that this beggarly world can give.² The apostle makes a challenge, which men nor devils could never accept or take up: "Who shall separate us from the love of Christ? shall tribulation, or distress, or persecution, or famine, or nakedness, or sword? Nay, in all these things we are more than conquerors through him that loved us."³ Nay, at death your portion would swim out with you in that shipwreck; death, which parts all other portions from men, will give you full possession of yours. Then, and not till then, you should know what it is worth; yea, even at the great day, the fire which shall burn up the world shall not so much as singe your portion. You might stand upon its ruins and sing, I have lost nothing; I have my portion, my inheritance, my happiness, my God still.

Other portions, like summer fruit, are soon ripe and soon rotten; but this portion, like winter fruit, though it be longer before the whole be gathered, yet it will continue. Gold and silver, in which other men's portion lies, are corruptible; but your portion, like the body of Christ, shall never see corruption.

When all earthly portions, as meat overdriven, certainly corrupts, or as water in cisterns quickly grows unsavory, this portion, like the water in Æsculapius's well, is not capable of putrefaction.

O friend, what are all the portions in the world, which, as a candle, consume in the use, and then go out in a stink, to this

---

1 1 John 2:13.
2 Romans 8:17.
3 Romans 8:35, 37.

eternal portion? It is reported of one Theodorus, that when there was music and feasting in his father's house, withdrew himself from all the company, and thus thought with himself: Here is content enough for the flesh; but how long will this last? This will not hold out long. Then falling on his knees, O Lord, my heart is open unto thee. I indeed know not what to ask, but only this, Lord, let me not die eternally. O Lord, thou knows I love thee; oh let me live eternally to praise thee. I must tell you, reader, to be eternally happy or eternally miserable, to live eternally or to die eternally, are of greater weight than you are aware of, yes, of far more concernment than you can conceive. Ponder this motive therefore thoroughly. God is not only a satisfying portion, filling every crevice of your soul with the light of joy and comfort; and a sanctifying portion, elevating your soul to its primitive and original perfection; and a universal portion; not health, or wealth, or friends, or honors, or liberty, or life, or house, or wife, or child, or pardon, or peace, or grace, or glory, or earth, or heaven, but all these and infinitely more; but also he is an eternal portion. This God would be your God for ever and ever.[1] Oh sweet word *ever!* you are the crown of the saints' crown, and the glory of their glory. Their portion is so full that they desire no more; they enjoy variety and plenty of delights above what they are able to ask or think, and want nothing but to have it fixed. May they but possess it in peace without interruption or cessation, they will trample all the kingdoms of the earth as dirt under their feet; and, lo! you are the welcome dove to bring this olive branch in your mouth, This God is our God for ever and ever. All the arithmetical figures of days, and months, and years, and ages, are nothing to this infinite cipher *ever*, which, though it stand for nothing in the vulgar account, yet contains

---

1 Psalm 48:14.

all our millions; yea, our millions and millions of millions are less than drops to this ocean *ever.*

If all the pleasures of the whole creation cannot countervail the fruition of God, though but for one moment, how happy should you be to enjoy him for ever! If the first fruits and foretastes of the Christian's felicity be so ravishing, what will the harvest be? Friend, little do you think what crowns, scepters, palms, thrones, kingdoms, glories, beauties, banquets, angelical entertainments, beatifical visions, societies, varieties, and eternities are prepared for them who choose God for their portion. If the saint's cross in the judgment of Moses—when at age, and able to make a true estimate of things—were more worth than all the treasures of Egypt, and he chose it rather, what is the saint's crown, eternal crown, worth?

To conclude this use, reader, take a serious view of this portion which is here tendered to you, and consider upon what easy terms it may be yours for ever. The portion is no less than the infinite God. "Behold, the nations are as a drop of the bucket, and are counted as the small dust of the balance: all nations before him are as nothing, and they are counted to him less than nothing, and vanity."[1] Other portions are bodily; he is spiritual, and so suitable to your soul. Other portions are mixed, like the Israelites' pillar, which had a dark as well as a light side; but he is pure; there is not the least spot in this sun; he is a sea of sweetness without the smallest drop of gall. Other portions are particular; there are some chinks in the outward man which they cannot fill, besides the many leaks of the soul, none of which they can stop; but he is a universal portion. All the excellencies of the creatures, even when their dregs and imperfections are removed, are but dark shadows of those many substantial excellencies which are in him.

1 Isaiah 40:15, 17.

He made all, he has all, he is all. The most fluent tongue will quickly be at a loss in extolling him, for he is above all blessing and praises. Other portions are debasing, like dross to gold, an allay to its worth; but he is an advancing portion, as a set of diamonds to a royal crown, infinitely adding to its value. Other portions are perishing; they may be lost; they will be left when death calls; your cloth will be then drawn, and not one dish remain on the table. But he is an everlasting portion. The souls that feast with him, like Mephibosheth at David's, eat bread at his table continually. "In his presence is fullness of joy, and at his right hand are pleasures for evermore."[1] Now, is not here infinite reason why you should choose this God for your portion?

Consider the terms upon which he is willing to be your portion. He desires no more than you would take him for your treasure and happiness. Surely such a portion is worthy of all acceptance. Be your own judge; may not God expect, and does he not deserve, as much respect as your earthly portion has had? Can your esteem of him be too high, or your love to him be too hot, or your labor for him too great? Oh what warm embraces have you given the world! Throw that strumpet now out of your arms, and take the fairest of ten thousand in her room. What high thoughts have you had of the world? What would you not formerly do or suffer to gain a little more of it? Now, pull down that usurper out of the throne, and set the King of saints there, whose place it is. Esteem him superlatively above all things, and make it your business, whatsoever he call you to do or suffer, to gain his love, which is infinitely better than life itself. Do but exalt him in your heart as your chiefest good, and in your life as your utmost end, and he will make a deed of gift of himself to you. Is it not rational what he

---

1 Psalm 16:11.

desires? Why should you then refuse? Here is God, there is the world; here is bread, there is husks; here is the substance, there is a shadow; here is paradise, there is an apple; here is fullness, there is emptiness; here is a fountain, there is a broken cistern; here is all things, there is nothing; here is heaven, there is hell; here is eternity, I say, eternity of joy and pleasure, there is eternity. O that word eternity, of sorrow and pain! Choose now which of the two you will take, and advise with yourself what word I shall bring again to him that sent me.[1]

FIFTHLY, COMFORT TO SUCH AS HAVE GOD FOR THEIR PORTION. The doctrine may be useful by way of consolation. It speaks much comfort to every true Christian—God is your portion. Your portion is not in toys and trifles, in narrow limited creatures, but in the blessed boundless God. He cannot be poor who has my lord mayor to his friend, much less he that has God to his portion—a portion so precious and perfect, that none of the greatest arithmeticians ever undertook to compute its worth, as knowing it impossible—a portion so permanent, that neither death, nor life, nor the world, nor principalities, nor powers, nor things present, nor things to come, can part you from it. This cordial may enliven you in a dying estate. None can part you and your portion. The winter may freeze the ponds, but not the ocean. All other portions may be frozen and useless in hard weather, but this portion is ever full and filling. Hagar, when her bottle of water was spent, wept, because she did not see the fountain that was so near her. The absence of the creatures need not make you mourn, who has the presence of the Creator.

You may have comfort from your portion in the most afflicted condition. Do men plunder you of your estate? You are rich towards God, and may suffer the spoiling of your goods

---
1 1 Chronicles 21:12.

joyfully, knowing that you have a more enduring substance.[1] Do they cast you into prison? Though your body be in fetters, your soul enjoys freedom. No chains can so fasten you to the earth, but you may mount up to heaven upon the wings of meditation and prayer. Do they take away your food? You have meat to eat which they know not of, and wine to drink which makes glad the heart of man.[2] Is your body sick? Your soul is sound, and so long all is well. The inhabitants shall not say, I am sick. The people that dwell therein shall be forgiven their iniquities. Is your life in danger? If your enemies kill you, they cannot hurt you; they will do you the greatest courtesy. They will do that kindness for you, for which you have many a time prayed, sighed, wept; even free you from your corruptions, and send you to the beatifical vision. When they call you out to die, they do but, as Christ to Peter, call you up to the mount, where you shall see your Saviour transfigured, and say, Let us build tabernacles. Oh, it is good to be here. Though Saul was frantic without a fiddler, and Belshazzar could not be cheerful without his cups, yet the philosopher could be merry, said Plato, without music, and much more the Christian under the greatest outward misery. What weight can sink him who has the everlasting arms to support him? What want can sadden him who has infinite bounty and mercy to supply him? Nothing can make him miserable who has God for his happiness. "Blessed is the people whose God is the Lord." O Christian, you may walk so that the world may know you are above their affrightments, and that all their allurements are below your hopes.

In particular, the doctrine is comfortable against the death of our Christian friends, and against our own deaths.

---
1 Hebrews 10:34.
2 Psalm 104:15.

First, It is a comfort against the death of our friends. God is a godly man's portion, therefore they are blessed who die in the Lord without us; and we are happy who live in the Lord without them.

It is a comfort that they are happy without creatures. What wise man will grieve at his friend's gain? In the ceremonial law there was a year of jubilee, in which every man who had lost or sold his land, upon the blowing of a trumpet had possession again. The death's-day of your believing relation is his day of jubilee, in which he is restored to the possession of his eternal and inestimable portion. Who ever pined that married an heir in his minority, at his coming to age, and going to receive his portion? Their death is not penal, but medicinal; not destructive, but perfective to their souls. It does that for them which none of the ordinances of God, nor providences of God, nor graces of the Spirit ever yet did for them. It sends the weary to their sweet and eternal rest. This serpent is turned into a rod, with which God works wonders for their good. The Thracians wept at the births of men, and feasted at their funerals. If they counted mortality a mercy, who could see death only to be the end of outward sufferings, shall not we who besides that see it to be the beginning of matchless and endless solace? A wife may well wring her hands, and pierce her heart with sorrow, when her husband is taken away from her, and dragged to execution, to hell; but surely she may rejoice when he is called from her by his prince, to live at court in the greatest honors and pleasures, especially when she is promised within a few days to be sent for to him, and to share with him in those joys and delights for ever.

Some observe that the Egyptians mourned longer (for they mourned seventy days) for old Jacob's death than Joseph his own son; and the reason is this, because they had hopes only in this life, when Joseph knew that, as his father's body was carried to the earthly, so his soul was translated to the heavenly Canaan. "I would not have you ignorant concerning them which are asleep, that ye sorrow not even as others that have no hope."[1]

As they are happy without us, for God is their portion; so we are happy without them. We have our God still; that stormy wind which blew out our candles, did not extinguish our sun. Our friend, when on his or her deathbed, might bespeak us, as Jacob his sons: "I die, but God shall visit you; I go from you, but God shall abide with you. I leave you, but God will find you; he will never leave you nor forsake you." Reader, if God live, though your friends die, I hope you are not lost, you are not undone. May not God say to you, when you are pining and whining for the death of your relations or friends, as if you were eternally miserable, as Elkanah to Hannah: "Am not I better to thee than ten sons?" Am not I better to you than ten husbands, than ten wives, than ten thousand worlds? Oh think of it, and take comfort in it!

Secondly, It is comfortable against your own death. God is your portion, and at death you shall take possession of your vast estate. Now you have a freehold in law, a right to it; but then you shall have a freehold in deed, make your entry on it, and be really seized of it. It is much that heathens who were purblind and could not see afar off into the joys and pleasures of the other world, the hopes of which alone can make death truly desirable, should with less fear meet this foe than many Christians. Nay, it was more difficult to persuade several of those pagans to live out all their days, than it is to persuade some amongst us to be willing to die when God calls them. Codrus could throw himself into a pit, that his country might live by his death. Cato could, against the entreaty of all his friends, with his own hands,

---

1 1 Thessalonians 4:13.

open the door at which his life went out.¹ Platinus, the philosopher, held mortality a mercy, that we might not always be liable to the miseries of this life. When the Persian king wept that all his army should die in the revolution of an age, Artabanus told him that they should all meet with so many and such great evils, that they should wish themselves dead long before. Lysimachus threatened to kill Theodorus, but he stoutly answered the king, that was no great matter, the cantharides, a little fly, could do as much. Cleombrotus having read Plato of the soul's immortality, did presently send his own soul out of his body to try and taste it. The bare opinion of the Druids, that the soul had a continuance after death, made them hardy in all dangers, said Caesar, and fearless of death.²

Christians surely have more cause to be valiant in their last conflict; and it is no credit to their Father that they are so loath to go home. The Turks tell us that surely Christians do not believe heaven to be so glorious a place as they talk of; for if they did, they would not be so unwilling to go thither. It may make the world think the child has but cold welcome at his father's house, that he lingers so much abroad; certainly such bring an ill report upon the good land.

Christian, what is it in death that you are afraid of? Is it not a departure, the jail delivery of a long prisoner, the sleep of your body, and a wakening of your soul, the way to bliss, the gate of life, the portal to paradise? Are you not sure to triumph before you fight, by dying to overcome death, and when you leave your body, to be joined to your head? The Roman general, in the encounter between Scipio and Hannibal, thought he could not use a more effectual persuasion to encourage his soldiers, than to tell them that they were to fight with those

---

1 Plutarch in Vit. Utic. Cat.
2 Cæs., lib. vi. De Bell. Gal.

whom they had formerly overcome, and who were as much their slaves as their enemies. You are to enter the list against that adversary whom you have long ago conquered in Jesus Christ, and who is more your slave than your enemy. Death is yours,[1] your servant and slave to help off your clothes, and to put you to your everlasting happy rest.

Is it the taking down of your earthly tabernacle which troubles you? Why, do you not know that death is the workman sent by the Father to pull down this earthly house of mortality and clay, that it may be set up anew, infinitely more lasting, beautiful, and glorious? Did you believe how rich and splendid he intends to make it, which cannot be unless taken down, you would contentedly endure the present toil and trouble, and be thankful to him for his care and cost. He takes down your vile body, that he may fashion it like to the glorious body of his own Son, which for brightness and beauty excels the sun in its best attire, far more than that does the meanest star.

Is it the untying of the knot betwixt body and soul which perplexes you? It is true they part; but, as friends going two several ways, shake hands till they return from their journey; they are as sure of meeting again as of parting; for your soul shall return laden with the wealth of heaven, and fetch his old companion to the participation of all his joy and happiness.

Is it the rotting of your body in the grave that grieves you? Indeed, Plato's worldling does sadly bewail it: Woe is me, that I shall lie alone rotting in the earth amongst the crawling worms, not seeing aught above, nor seen. But you who have read it is a sweet bed of spices for thy body to rest in, all the dark night of this world's duration, may well banish such fears. Have you never heard God speaking to you, as once to Jacob, "Fear not to go down into (Egypt, into) the grave, I will go down with

---

1 1 Corinthians 3:22.

thee, and I will bring thee up again."[1]

Besides, your soul shall never die. The heathen historian could comfort himself against death with this weak cordial, *Non omnis moriar,* All of me does not die; though my body be mortal, my books are immortal. But you have a stronger julep, a more rich cordial to clear your spirits; when your body fails, your soul will flourish. Thy death is a burnt-offering; when your ashes fall to the earth, the celestial flame of your soul will mount up to heaven. Farther, death will ease you of those most troublesome guests, which make your life now so burdensome; as the fire to the three children did not so much as singe or sear their bodies, but it burnt and consumed their bands, so death would not the least hurt your body or soul, but it would destroy those fetters of sin and sorrow, in which you are entangled. Besides, the sight of the blessed God, which is the only beatifical vision, which at death your soul shall enjoy.[2] Popish pilgrims take tedious journeys, and are put to much hardship and expense to behold a dumb idol. The queen of Sheba came from far to see Solomon, and hear his wisdom; and will you not take a step from earth to heaven—in a moment, in the twinkling of an eye, your journey will be gone, and your work be done—to see Jesus Christ, a greater than Solomon? Have you not many a time prayed long, and cried for it? Have you not trembled lest you should miss it? Has not your heart once and again leaped with joy in hope of it? And when the hour is come, and you are sent for, do you shrink back? For shame, Christian; walk worthy of your calling, and quicken your courage in your last conflict. As the Jews, when it thunders and lightens, open their windows, expecting the Messias should come. Oh when the storm of death beats upon your body,

---

1 Genesis 46:4.
2 Nazianzen's Orations.

with what joy may you set those casements of your soul, faith and hope, wide open, knowing that your dearest Redeemer, who went before to prepare a place for you, will then come and fetch you to himself; that where he is, there you may be also, and that for ever.

Sermon 4

It Is Good for Me to Draw Near to God

By William Guthrie

But it is good for me to draw near to God.—Psalm 73:28.

These words are a part of the result of a very strange exercise, which a godly man had, being much stumbled, and troubled in heart at the prosperity of the wicked; because they got so much of their will in the world.— But now having surmounted the temptation, and got a second view of all things, relating both to the prosperity of the wicked, and to the afflicted condition of the godly, in contemplation of which, he resolves to draw near to God; *It is good*, says he, *to draw near to God.* As if he had said, I believe I am neither wise, nor happy to intermeddle so much with these things; and I know well it is my best to *draw near to God.* It is good for me to flee in unto him, and, as it were, to look out at my windows, until I see how all things here will roll. Now there is no great difficulty here, in the words now read, but what we may reach in the doctrine. We may consider them, either,

First, Simply, or absolutely; or,

Secondly, As they have a reference upon what goes before in the same place, or portion of Scripture. And,

First, Consider these words simply or absolutely, from

whence for doctrine we observe.

DOCTRINE. *That it is good to draw near to God; or good by way of eminency; it is truly and really good. It is an advantageous good. And it is enough for confirmation of the doctrine, that it is not only positively asserted here in the text, but it is also commanded as our duty by the apostle James.* "Draw nigh unto God, and he will draw nigh unto you."[1]

Now, in speaking to this, we shall,

I. Show you what it is to draw near unto God.

II. Show you what are the advantages of drawing near to God, or it is good to do so.

I. To show you what it is to draw near unto God. And,

1. A man should make his peace with God, in, and through the Mediator Jesus Christ; for until once that be done, a man may be said to be far from God; and there is a partition-wall standing betwixt God and him. It is the same with that advice given by Eliphaz to Job: *Acquaint now thyself with God, and be at peace with him, and so good shall come unto thee.*[2] Be friends with God, and all shall be well with you. You must come up unto some measure of conformity to the blessed will of God, and quit that life of estrangement from him, as is evident from that forecited text, *Draw nigh unto God, and he shall draw nigh unto you.* And this is explained in the words following: *Cleanse your hands, ye sinners; and purify your hearts, ye double-minded:* that is, Quit that filthy life of estrangement from God, in being more conformed unto him, and his will, as he has revealed unto you in his Word.

2. It is to seek more after communion, and fellowship with God; and to pursue after intimacy and familiarity with him; and to have more of his blessed company with us in

---

1 James 4:8.
2 Job 22:21.

our ordinary walk and conversation; according to that word, *Blessed are the people, that know the joyful sound: they shall walk, O Lord, in the light of thy countenance.*[1] This is to walk through the day, having a good understanding between God and us; and so to be always near unto him in keeping still up communication with him. And,

3. As it stands here in the text, it is the expression of one who has made up his peace already, and is on good terms with God; and differs a little from what the words absolutely imply; and so we may take it thus,

(1.) It implies the confirming, or making sure our interest in God, and so it supposes the man's peace to be made with God; for whoever be the author of this Psalm, it supposes he had made his peace; and therefore in the following words, it is subjoined, *I have put my trust in the Lord,* etc. that is, I have trusted my soul unto God, and made my peace with him through a Mediator. It is good whatever comes, it is always good to be near unto God that way, and to be made sure in him.

(2.) It implies to be more and more conformed unto the image of God, and therefore this nearness to him is opposed to that of being far from God. It is good, says he, to draw near to God in my duty; when so many are far from him.

(3.) It implies that which I was hinting at before, to lay by all things in the world; and to seek fellowship and communion with God; and to be more set apart for his blessed company: and to walk with him in a dependence upon him, as the great Burden-bearer; as him who is to be all in all unto us. In a word, to draw near unto God, is to make our peace with him; and to secure, and confirm that peace with him; and to study a conformity unto him; and to be near unto him in our walk

---

1 Psalm 89:15.

and conversation; in our fellowship, and whole carriage, and deportment to be always near unto him.

II. We come to the advantages, or how it is said, that it is good, and advantageous to draw near to God. We say, it is said to be good to draw near unto God. It is good to take good in that way. It is good in its self; and it is good in respect of the happy consequences that follow upon it.

1. It is a pleasant good. *Wisdom's ways are pleasantness; and all her paths are peace.*[1] And although many of you think that the people of God have a sorrowful, and sad life of it; yet this flows not from their nearness unto God; but it is, because they depart out of his way, or step aside from following him.

2. As it is good in itself, and a pleasant good; so it is a creditable and honorable good. Is it not good to be at peace, and in good terms with God; to be conformed unto his will, which is the supreme rule of all righteousness; and to have intimate fellowship with him? We would think it a very honorable thing, to be in favor, and on good terms with a man that rules over all nations; supposing him to be a good man, and that our intimacy with him were not scandalous, and offensive. But it is quite another thing to be in favor, and on good terms with him who rules over all laws and all men as so many insects; under whom the inhabitants of the earths appear as so many grasshoppers in his sight.

O but it is good in respect of the circumstances and consequences of it, and so it is also a profitable good.—Yea, it secures a man's soul, and eternal well-being. It keeps him in perfect peace. It has many testificates and outlettings of God's countenance, which is better unto him than barns full of corn, or cellars full of wine and oil. Yea he is all good, *The Lord will give grace and glory, and will withhold no good thing from*

---
1 Proverbs 3:17.

them that walk uprightly.[1] And who are these? Even such as are near unto God. So that it is a good thing to draw near unto him.

USE. Would you be for ever happy in the enjoying of that which is supremely good? Well then, draw near unto God. Every one readily follows after some thing that he thinks to be good.[2] There are many that say, Who will show us any good. The most part would be at some visible or seeming good. Yes, but this is a more sure and permanent good, that will fill your hand. Then go, and acquaint yourselves. Seek to have communion with him, and to be confirmed and conformed unto him. In prosecuting of this use, we shall speak a word unto these sorts of people.

1. To some who are wholly estranged from God, (although I know there are many of that will not take with this charge.) Go and acquaint yourselves with him, if you would be for ever happy. And what is this but to know him, and an offer of yourselves unto him? How is it that you make your acquaintance with one come from France, or so, having some knowledge of him, and expecting great favor at his hand? You offer your service unto him, if it should be unto the tenth generation. But have you done so unto the God of heaven? You will make your court to man in such a matter, and will you not draw near to God? You will do it the better, when you know how far heaven and you are from one another. For your better understanding of this, I will give you a few marks of those who are far from him.

(1.) Have you known any thing of his voice. You will say, If I were near such a one, I would know his voice. If you do not, you are yet far from him. *My sheep hear my voice, and I know*

---
1 Psalm 84:11.
2 Psalm 4:6.

them, and they follow me. What God speaks in this gospel is foolishness unto many; but those who are his sheep know his voice, and unto them this gospel is the wisdom and the power of God. Could you never lay claim unto that word. *It is the voice of my beloved that knocketh,*[1] etc. I know whose voice it is. Were you never persuaded that this gospel was the most wise of all devices that ever was contrived, or thought upon to save sinners? This is to his voice. You that count the preaching of the gospel but babbling, you are far from God in hearing of his voice, and cannot but expect to stumble upon what you hear concerning him.

(2.) Know ye his face? Who is he that says, Stay till I be near unto him, and then perhaps I shall know him? But if you do not know his face, you are far from him.—And yet I persuaded that there are many hearing me, that know not what I mean. But pose yourselves. Know ye any thing of the difference betwixt the smiles and frowns of God? Or what it is to have your hearts and souls warmed with the heat and light of his countenance? Has your soul ever been made to weep within you with his love? If not, it is a bad token; for the people of God know his face; and whenever they hear him named, their affections go out after him.

(3.) What dealings have you in your ordinary way and walk with God? Do you acknowledge him in all your ways? He knows the wicked afar off, and has no dealings with them. Do you venture upon nothing without God's counsel? Do you keep your eye upon him in your ordinary business? And do you give an account thereof unto him? If it is so, it is well. But if you have no mind of God; only when you put on your clothes, and wash your hands, it may be you retire a little in secret; and then lose any thought you have had of him all the

---

1 Song of Solomon 5:2.

day long; that is a bad token that you are yet far from God: and if death shall meet with you in this situation, your hearts shall be roughly handled by it.

2. The second sort that I would speak unto are, those who are truly godly. Would you be happy and good in the land of the living; then draw near to God in all these respects formerly noticed. And that you may do it, it were good for you, that,

(1.) You were convinced of your being in a great measure far from God; and in that respect unlike what I formerly spoke of. I believe there be many of you that are not well seen yet in your interest in God. Then if you would be clear in this, *draw near unto God*, and resolve on what will be well pleasing to him. And what is that? It is even to remove whatever stands betwixt him and you. When you go unto prayer, or when you would lay claim unto any promise; then *do not regard sin in your heart*. Put away all idols of jealousy. Let none of them come in with you before the Lord; for if you do, he will never regard your desires in prayer: and this is a time wherein there are many loose hands in this respect. Therefore it were good for you to step home, and be sure where you are to take up your lodging at night.

(2.) Study to be convinced, that you are by nature far from God, and in your walk and conversation, from that communion with him that you might attain unto, even while here.—And if once you were at that, you would think it your unquestionable duty to *draw near unto God*, in all these respects before mentioned. But where is that labor of love, that unweariedness in duty, and that disposition to suffer every thing for Christ? Are not all these, in a great measure, gone? What fainting, failing, and scarring at the cross? So that but scratch the clothes of many Christians, and they will be like to go besides themselves. Where is that appetite and desire after Christ, and his righteousness, which folk sometimes so vigorously pursued? Where is that estimation of, and enquiry after marks of grace in the soul, that has sometimes been? How perilous has a mark of grace sometimes been, and how did it alarm you when it was observed? And where is that sympathy, and longing for the discovery of duty, submission unto reproof, that were wont to be amongst you? Are you not rather afraid to hear your duty laid out before you? And where is that simplicity of the gospel, or that happiness people had in hearing the gospel, when they had not such skill to shift, or evade the word, and to put all by, except those sentences that pleased their own fancy? and when they dare not entertain a challenge of conscience all night, but it behoved them to mourn for it before the Lord, until it was removed. Has not many of you got the devil's wisdom to lodge a challenge all night, and not be troubled with it? And where is that tenderness of conscience, that would have made people abstain from every appearance of evil, and would have made them walk circumspectly in regard of offenses, and mourn for them before God? And where is that true zeal for the interest of Christ that was once in our corporations in these dominions? Is not that gone, and is there any rightly exercised, when they see the matters of God going wrong?—Now you should draw near unto God in all these things. Now,

(3.) Is there any pursuing after this nearness unto God that was wont sometimes to have been a case of conscience? But now to mend our evil faults, of all cases this is the most remote from us. I say, so to speak, it is far to the sheaf here. The time has been when you would not have been satisfied, if God had not been drawing out your hearts after him, or lying, as it were, all night, *as a bundle of myrrh, between your breasts*. But, oh! is not this almost gone? O therefore draw near to him. Again, it is good, as we commonly say, to come to old use and wont again, if you come no farther. But,

Secondly, I come to speak of the words as they have a reference unto what goes before the text. And,

First. They turn upon this—He had seen the wicked prosper and get much of their will in the world. When he beheld this, he was made to stumble at it; but after recollecting, and considering it a little, he recovers himself, and begins to speak of what he had formerly said concerning it. And here, says he, *It is good for me to draw near unto God.* Whence I observe,

1. That a godly man's heart should satisfy itself, over all the prosperity the wicked has, or can have in the world; and therefore the word in the original imports a gaining *of God unto me.* It is good for me; it is an only good for me, to draw near to God, and that is enough to satisfy me, over all, and beyond all the prosperity of the wicked in the world. And so much is insinuated, *of the wicked that prosper in his way.*[1] What should we then do? Why, trust in God. Be satisfied in him as your blessed choice and portion. And the grounds on which a godly man's heart should satisfy itself over all that he sees in the lot of the wicked, are these,

(1.) The fountain itself is better than any drops that come to the wicked. God himself is better than the creature. He is better than ten sons, yea he is better far than any good thing that proceeds from him. Therefore, he says, in the words preceding the text, *Whom have I in the heavens but thee, and there is none on the earth that I desire besides thee.* When he has counted all, this is the sum of the whole reckoning.

(2.) He goes further on the same ground. As if he would say, I see that all their folk, *viz.* the wicked, *stand on slippery places.* I would not be in their place for all that they enjoy, and as much to it. But as for me, *Thou wilt guide me with thy*

---

1 Psalm 37:7.

counsel, and afterwards receive me unto glory. No other good thing, is so good as God. God is good in himself; and he commands all that is really good unto that man that draws near unto him, even from his shoe latchet unto the salvation of his soul; and makes every thing turn to him, as it were, in the hollow of his hand. *The Lord will give grace, and glory, no good thing will he withhold from them that walk uprightly.*[1] And may not that satisfy us fully?

For Use 1. This reproves the godly, who grudge and fret at the prosperity of the wicked. *Fret not thyself because of evil doers.*[2] Simple poor folk, simple fools would he say, they will have little enough yet to leave.—But the believer's portion is far preferable unto theirs. It is an only good. It is better than many portions. O learn to compare your lot with the lot of the men of this world. Count, and count on, and see whose number exceeds. Tell, and tell over, and see who tells longest; for there is much counting in your lot, compared to what is in theirs. That is a strange word, *Was not Esau Jacob's brother; saith the Lord: Yet loved Jacob, hated Esau, and laid his mountain and heritage waste.*[3] Esau had the dominion for a time, yet the headship or superiority belonged unto Jacob. And that might satisfy him, thought he had not so much worldly substance as Esau. Believers may sing that song with David, when near his end, *Although my house be not so ordered with God, yet he hath made with me an everlasting covenant, ordered in all things sure,*[4] etc.

Use 2. Although there be a party of wicked men, men of Belial, that have to do with in the world; a party that are like

---

1 Psalm 84:11.
2 Psalm 37:1.
3 Malachi 1:2, 3.
4 2 Samuel 23:5.

briers and thorns; so that the people of had need of gauntlet gloves, when dealing with them; yet the covenant is for that also: for *this is all my salvation, and all desire;* although he make it not to grow.

2. Observe, That the more the wicked get their will, the people of God should still draw the more near unto God. And this is imported in Psalm 37:3, *Trust in the Lord, and do good;—delight thyself also in the Lord.* This is opposed unto fretting at the prosperity of the wicked: This is the duty of all the godly, the wicked get most of their desires in the world; and that for these reasons.

(1.) Because they may be satisfied in so doing. Do the wicked get much of their mind in their lot and portion? Well, the people of God should fill themselves full of their portion: for there is a reality in it: but there is none in the portion of the wicked. What are houses, lands, gold, silver, or ease, to eternal life? O take a draught thereof, by drawing near unto God.—And,

(2.) Because your trials and temptations are coming. And if the wicked get up and have the dominion, as it is likely they may; then the godly may make for their sheet and their shoes, if they can come at them.

(3.) Because this is the way to preserve you, and to guard your hearts from mistakes, when you with the temptation this man met with. A sad temptation; when godly folk get not their will in what they would be at, for God and his interest: and godless folk get their will and design. Then they are ready to misrepresent, and mistake the voice of providence. You see this godly man accounted himself as a beast under this. But a drawing near unto God will prevent every mistake in this case.—And,

(4.) Because whenever the wicked get most of their will,

that prognosticates some great revolution in the land. But at the same time it is also true, that it is, *that they may be cut off, and destroyed for ever.* Then may the Lord save the innocent; for there will be stirs. Therefore flee into your windows. Draw near unto God.

USE 1. You hear what is your duty, when wicked folk get most of their designs and commands over all. Here it is; draw near unto God; and thus hold you out of harms way in an evil time.

USE 2. See how you may be put into a capacity for a day of trial, and be creditably carried through. And if you would be even with wicked men, and guard against mistakes, and be enabled to be faithful, and forth-coming for, or to God, then draw near unto him in all he has commanded you.

USE 3. This reproves those who are resolving to take another way; and cast about to the leeward, and row to the shore, to see what friends they may have at court; to curry the favor of great men; to get their own business well managed; and to tell ill tales of the godly. Be sure you shall meet with a mischief. It is good at all times, but especially at such a time, to draw near unto God.—And if you do not this, you shall never have safety in any other way. But,

Secondly. Take the words as they are an inference from these words before the text, in the 25TH verse; *Whom have I in heaven, but thee; and there is none upon earth that I desire besides thee: my heart and my flesh faileth me,* etc. Here we see the Psalmist very near unto God; and yet in the text, he says, *It is good for me to draw near unto God.* Whence

I observe, Let a man be as near unto God as he can imagine, yet it is good to draw near unto him, and to seek to have nearer fellowship and more intimate acquaintance with him. This man was near, yet he seeks to be nearer unto him; even to have his arms full of God (so to speak); and the reason is,

1. Because the life of true religion in the world, is but a strong appetite, and a heart hungering after God.—And therefore folk should still be hungering, and seeking after more from him. And,

2. Because even that which you have got, you cannot keep, unless you be still in the pursuit of more. You lose what you have got, and scatter as fast as you have gathered; if you be not still making progress and increase. Therefore, *Hold up my going in thy path, that my footsteps slip not.*[1] That is, hold a grip of me, otherwise I will suddenly go wrong. You will come unto a small reckoning, if you draw not near, and more near unto God.

USE 1. This serves for trial of your reception of God. Try if you be still pursuing after more. You that think you have got something from God, and are sitting down upon that, I am in doubt whether that reception of God be at all real. For where it is real, it still puts the soul upon longing for more. If your reception of God put you not upon working for more, it is a bad token, and says that either you are not sure; or else there is some dead flea in the pot of ointment.

USE 2. And you that have really got any thing of God; work fast for more: study to go forward; otherwise I defy you to keep what you have already gotten. The devil will get his hand upon it; and then you will be in hazard of losing what you have once gotten.

USE 3. *Open your mouths wide, and the Lord will fill them abundantly.* There are treasures of good things with him, that you never yet beheld, or lighted upon; sweet fills of love, peace, joy; perfect victory over sin; self-denial, and dying to the world, being alive to nothing but Christ, being filled with all

---

1 Psalm 17:5.

the fullness of God. All these, and much more are to be had for the seeking after.

Thirdly, Consider the words, as they are connected with these immediately preceding the text. *Thou hast destroyed all that go a-whoring from thee.* Hence observe,

That it is good to draw near unto God; the only way in all the world, to secure a man from the dreadful judgments that are coming upon wicked men, is to draw near to God. This is the only way: this is to foresee the evil, and run, and hide yourselves. *Flee under the shadow of the Almighty.*[1] This is the only place for shelter against the judgments of God that have been long impending over us, are now dropping, and will at last be rained upon us. Then let us draw near unto God.

USE 1. It were good that folk considered, and were oftener thinking upon those judgments that are to be poured out upon wicked men. There was a generation of ungodly men in Scotland that were enemies to the people of God; and many of them are yet alive. God has dropped dreadful judgments on some of them, and yet continues to drop them upon the rest; and it is likely the dregs of the cup will be the bitterest?—You may believe it, you that are the people of God have no other way to escape the judgments of God, but by drawing near unto him. Fancy not an immunity from judgment another way.—There is a sword of the Lord that will cut off the wicked; and the righteous have no way of escape, but by drawing near unto God. And if you would set yourselves seriously to it, God would meet you midway, and more; as it is evident from the forecited text, James 4:8.

USE 2. It were good for all God's people in times of temptation and trials, to follow this godly man's example here. He has been in a temptation, and he wrestles with it and carries off the

---
1 Psalm 91:1.

spoil of the temptation, as it were, upon the edge of his hat, and comes off the field honorably.—Finally, Study to carry in this way whenever a temptation comes upon you, and you are engaged in it. Thus bring some of the honorable spoil of the temptation with you. It is good for me to draw near unto God.

Sermon 5

IT IS GOOD TO DRAW NEAR TO GOD

By Hugh Binning

But it is good for me to draw near to God: I have put my trust in the Lord God, that I may declare all thy works.—PSALM 73:28.

After man's first transgression, he was shut out from the tree of life, and cast out of the garden, by which was signified his seclusion and sequestration from the presence of God, and communion with him: and this was in a manner the extermination of all mankind in one, when Adam was driven out of paradise. Now, this had been an eternal separation for any thing that we could do, (for we can do nothing but depart by a perpetual backsliding, and make the distance every day wider) except it had pleased the Lord, of his infinite grace, to condescend to draw near to us in gracious promises and offers of a Redeemer. If he had not made the first journey from heaven to earth, by sending his only Sun, we should have given over the hope of returning from earth to heaven. But he has taken away the greatest part of that distance, in drawing near to our nature; yea, in assuming our flesh into the fellowship of his glorious divinity. He has stooped so low to meet with us, and offered himself the trusting place between God and us, a fit meeting-place, where there is a conjunction of the interests of both parties, and now, there is no more to do, but to draw near to God in Jesus Christ, since he has made the great journey to come down to us. We have not that infinite gulf of satisfaction to justice to pass over; we have not the height of divine Majesty, as he is infinitely above us, and offended with us, to climb up unto. Certainly we could not but fall into the lake that is below us, if we were to aim so high. But the Lord has been pleased to descend to us, in our mean capacity in the flesh, and fill up the immeasurable gulf of justice by the infinite merits and sufferings of his Son in our flesh. And now he invites us, he requests us, to come to him in his Son and have life. We are not come to Mount Sinai, that might not be touched, that burnt with fire and tempest, where there were terrible sights and intolerable noises. I say, such a God we might have had to do with, a consuming fire, instead of an instructing light—a devouring fire, instead of a healing Sun of righteousness, considering that there is nothing in us which is not fit and prepared fuel for everlasting burnings. But we are come—and that is the eternal wonder of angels—unto Mount Sion, to be citizens in the city of God, and fellow-citizens with blessed angels and glorified spirits, to peace and reconciliation with him who was our judge. And if you ask how this may be? I answer, because we have one Jesus, the Mediator of the new covenant, to come to, whose blood cries louder for pardon of sinners than all men's transgressions can cry for punishment of sinners.[1]

Let us then consider the first step and degree of union with God—it consists in faith in Jesus Christ. This is the first motion of the soul in drawing near to God; for, as there is no remission without blood, so no access to God without a mediator. For if you consider what is in Jesus Christ, you will find that which

1 Hebrews 12:18–20.

will engage the desire of the heart; as also that which will give boldness and confidence to act that desire. Eternal life is promised and proposed in him—he offers rest to weary souls, and has it to give. That which we ignorantly and vainly seek elsewhere, here it is to be found. For personal excellencies, he is the chief infinitely beyond comparison; and for suitableness to us and our necessities, all the gospel is an expression of it; so that he is presented in the most attractive drawing manner that can be imagined. And then, when the desires are inflamed, yet if there be no oil of hope to feed it, it will soon cool again. Therefore, take a view again, and you may have boldness to enter into the holiest by the blood of Jesus. There was some kind of distance kept in the Old Testament—none but the high priest might enter into the holiest place: but the entry of our High Priest into it, that is, into heaven, has made it patent to all that come to him and apply his blood. There is a new and living way by the holy flesh of Christ, consecrated and made, of infinite value and use, by the divinity of his person; and, therefore, having such a one of our kindred so great with God, we may draw near with a true heart and full assurance of faith, having our consciences sprinkled, etc.[1] Now, since the way is made plain to you, and the entry is opened up in the gospel, do you not find your hearts stir within you to draw near to him? Do you not find a necessity of making peace by such a Mediator? O that you knew the great distance between God and your natures, and what the hazard is, "Lo! they that are far from thee shall perish": then certainly you would take hold of this invitation, and be easily drawn unto Jesus Christ. But unto you who have adventured to draw near for pardon of sin in Christ, I would recommend unto you, that you would draw yet nearer to God. After that the partition-wall of wrath

---

1 Hebrews 10:18–20, etc.

and condemnation is removed, yet there is much darkness in your minds, and corruption in your natures, that separates from him; I mean, intercepts and disturbs that blessed communion you are called unto. Therefore, I would exhort you, as James, "Draw near to God, and he will draw near to you,"[1] and that, wherein this most consists, is in studying that purification of our natures, that cleansing of our hearts from guile; and our hands from offenses, by which our souls may draw towards a resemblance of God. This access and drawing near to God in assimilation and conformity of nature, is the great design of the gospel. "Be ye holy, for I am holy." Now, you are agreed, walk with him,[2] as Enoch "walked with God,"[3] that is, labor in all your conversation to set him before your eyes, and to study to be well-pleased with him in all things, and to please him in all, to conform yourselves to his pleasure in every thing. And this communion in walking especially consists in that communication of the spirit with God in prayer: this is the nearest and sweetest approach when the soul is lifted up to God, and is almost out of itself in him; and this being the ordinary exercise and motion of the soul, it exceedingly advances in the first point of nearness, that is, in conformity with God. Drawing often near in communion with him in prayer, makes the soul draw towards his likeness, even as much converse of men together will make them like one another.

Now, for the commendation of this, "It is good." What greater evil can be imagined than separation from the greatest good? And what greater good, than accession to the greatest good? Every thing is in so far happy and well, as it is joined with, and enjoys, that which is convenient for it. Light is the

---

1 James 4:8.
2 Amos 3:3.
3 Genesis 5:22.

perfection of the earth; remove it, and what a disconsolate and unpleasant thing is it! Now, truly there is nothing suitable to the immortal spirit of man but God; and, therefore, all its happiness or misery must be measured by the access or recess, nearness or distance, of that infinite goodness. Therefore, is it any wonder, that all they that go a-whoring from him perish, as every man's heart does? For we are infinitely bound by creation, by many other bonds stronger than wedlock, to consecrate and devote ourselves wholly to God; but this is treacherously broken. Every man turns aside to vanity and lies, and is guilty of heart-whoredom from God, and spiritual idolatry, because the affection that should be preserved chaste for him is prostitute to every base object. So then, this divorcement of the soul from God cannot but follow thereupon, even an eternal eclipse of true and real life and comfort. And whoever draws back from the fountain of life and salvation, cannot but find elsewhere perdition and destruction.[1] My beloved, let us set thus aside all other things which are the pursuits and endeavors of the most part of men. Men's natural desires are carried towards health, food, raiment, life and liberty, peace, and such like; but, the more rational sort of men seek after some shadow of wisdom and virtue. Yet the generality of men, both high and low, have extravagant illuminated desires towards riches, pleasure, preferment; and all that we have spoken is enclosed within the narrow compass of men's abode here, which is but for a moment. So that, if it were possible that all these aforementioned desires and delights of men could attend any man for the space of an hundred years, though he had the concurrence of the streams of the creatures to bring him in satisfaction, though all the world should bow to him and be subject to the beck of his authority without stroke of sword, though

---

1 Hebrews 10 ult.

all the creatures should spend their strength and wit upon his satisfaction; yet do but consider what that shall be within some few years, when he shall be spoiled of all that attendance, denuded of all external comforts, when the fatal period must close his life, peace, health, and all; and his poor soul also, that was drowned in that gulf of pleasure, shall then find itself robbed of its precious treasure, that is, God's favor, and so remain in everlasting banishment from his presence. Do you think, I say, that man were happy? Nay! O happy Lazarus, who is now blessed in Abraham's bosom, who enjoys an eternity of happiness for a moment's misery! But, my beloved, you know that it is not possible even to attain to that imagined happiness here. All the gain that is found is not able to quit the cost and expense of grief, vexation, care, toiling and sweating that is about them.

But if you would be persuaded, there is that to be found easily, which you trouble yourselves seeking elsewhere; and believe me, though the general apprehension of men be—that peace, plenty, preferment, and satisfaction in this life, to compense their pains, are more easily attainable than fellowship and communion with God; yet I am persuaded that there is nothing more practicable than the life of religion. God has condemned the world under vanity and a curse, and that which is crooked can by no art or strength be made straight; but he has made this attainable by his gracious promises, even a blessed life, in approaching near to himself, the fountain of all life. And this is a certain good, an universal good, and an eternal good. It will not disappoint you as other things do, of which you have no assurance for all your toilings. This is made more infallible to a soul that truly seeks it in God. It is as certain that they cannot be ashamed through frustration, as that he is faithful. And then it is an universal good, one comprehensive of all, one eminently and virtually all things created, to be joined to the infinite all-fullness of God. This advances the soul to a participation of all that is in him. This is health.[1] This is light.[2] It is life,[3] liberty,[4] food and raiment,[5] and what not? It is profit, pleasure, preferment, in the superlative degree, and not scattered in so many various streams, which divide and distract the heart, but all combined in one. It is the true good of both soul and body, and so the only good of man. And lastly, it is eternal, to be coetaneous[6] with your soul. Of all other things it may be said, "I have seen an end of them," they were and are not. But this will survive time, and all the changes of it, and then it will begin to be perfect, when all perfection is at an end. Now, from all this, I would exhort you in Jesus Christ to ponder those things in your hearts, and consider them in reference to your own souls, that you may say with David, "It is good for me to draw near to God."

That which all men seek after is happiness and well-being. Men pursue nothing but under the notion of good; and to complete that which may be called good, there is required some excellency in the thing itself, and then a conveniency and suitableness to us, and these jointly draw the heart of man. But the great misery is, that there is so much ignorance and misapprehension of that which is truly good, and then, when any thing of it is known, there is so little serious consideration and application of it to ourselves; and this makes the most part of men wander up and down in the pursuit of divers things;

---

1 Psalm 42:11; Proverbs 3:8.
2 John 8:12.
3 John 11:25.
4 John 8:36.
5 Isaiah 61:10, and John 4:14.
6 Coetaneous—of the same age; beginning to exist at the same time; contemporaneous.—*Webster's 1913 Dictionary.*

which are not that true good of the soul, and set their hearts on that which is not, until they find their hearts fall down as wanting a foundation, and then they turn about again to some other vanity. And so the wanderings and strayings of men are infinite, because the by-ways are innumerable, though the true way be but one. Yea, the turnings and toilings of one man are various and manifold, because he quickly loses the scent of happiness in every way he falls into, and therefore must turn to another. And thus men are never at any solid setting about this great business, never resolute wherein this happiness consists, nor peremptory to follow it; but they fluctuate upon uncertain apprehensions, and diverse affections, until the time and date of salvation expire; and then they must know certainly and surely the inevitable danger and irrecoverable loss they have brought themselves to, who would not take notice of the sure way, both of escaping wrath and attaining happiness while it was to be found.

Well, then, this is the great business we have here to do; yea, to make the circle the larger, it is that great business we have to do in this world, to know wherein the true well-being and eternal welfare of our souls consist, and by any means to apply unto that, as the only thing necessary, in regard of which, all other things are ceremonies, circumstances, and indifferent things. And to guide us in this examination and application, here is one man, who, having almost made shipwreck upon the rocks which men commonly dash upon, and being by the Lord led safely by, and almost arrived at the coast of true felicity, he sets out a beacon, and lights a candle to all who shall follow him, to direct them which way they shall steer their course. Examples teach more effectually than rules. It is easy for every man to speak well upon this point in general, and readily all will acknowledge that here it is, and nowhere else. But yet all this is outcried by the contrary noise of every man's practice. These general grants of truth are recalled in the conversations of men, therefore they cannot have much influence upon any man. But when we hear one speak, and see him walk so too; when we have the example of a most wise man, who wanted not these worldly expectations which other men have, so that he not only propones it to us, but after much serious advisement, after mature consideration of all that can be said of the wicked's best estate, and the godly's worst, setting down resolute conclusions for himself—"It is good for me to draw near to God"; yea, so determinate in it, that if none of the world should be of that mind, he would not change it—though all should walk in other ways, he would choose to be rather alone in this, than in the greatest crowd of company in any other. Now, I say, when we have such a copy cast us, a man of excellent parts in sobriety and sadness, choosing that way, which all in words confess to be the best; should not this awake us out of our dreams, and raise us up to some more attention and consideration of what we are doing? The words, you see, are the holy resolution of a holy heart, concerning that which is the chiefest good. You see the way to happiness, and you find the particular application of that to David's soul, or of his soul to it. We shall speak a word of the thing itself, then of the commendation of it, then of the application of it.

For the thing itself—drawing near to God—it gives us some ground to take a view of the posture in which men are found by nature, far off from God. Our condition by nature I cannot so fitly express, as in the apostle's words, "Without Christ, aliens from the commonwealth of Israel, strangers from the covenants of promise, having no hope, and without God in the world."[1] A deplorable estate indeed, hopeless and

1 Ephesians 2:12.

helpless! No hope in it; that is the extremity of misery, the refuse of all conditions. "Without Christ, and without God." Oh! these are words of infinite weight: without those, without whom it is simply impossible to be happy; and without whom it is not possible but to be miserable—without the fountain of light, life, and consolation, without which there is nothing but pure darkness, without any beam of light; nothing but death, without the least breathing of life; nothing but vexation, without the least drop of consolation. In a word, without these, and wanting these, whom, if you want, it were good to be spoiled of all being; to be nothing, if that could be, or never to have been any thing. Men will seek death, and cannot find it. O what a loss and deprivement is the loss of God, which makes death more desirable than life; and not to be at all, infinitely preferable to any being! Now, it is true, that the bringing in of multitudes within the pale of the visible church, is some degree of access and nearness to God; for then they become citizens as to eternal right, in the commonwealth of the church, and have the offers of the promises made to them; in respect of which visible standing, the apostle speaks of the whole church of Ephesus, "but now ye are made near who were far off,"[1] notwithstanding, that many of them were found afterwards to have left their first love.[2] But yet, beloved, to speak more inwardly, and as your souls stand in the sight of God, the generality of those who are near hand in outward ordinances are yet far off from God in reality—"without God and without Christ," as really, as touching any soul-feeling, as those who are altogether without. The bond of union and peace was broken in paradise; sin dissolved it, and broke off that nearness and friendship with God; and from that day to

---

1 Ephesians 2:13.
2 Revelation 2:4.

this day, there has been an infinite distance and separation betwixt man and God. The steps and degrees of it are many. There is darkness and blindness in men's minds. Such ignorance naturally possesses the multitude, that it wholly alienates them from the life of God.[1] For what fellowship can light, that pure light, have with such gross darkness as is among us? This certainly is the removal of that Sun of Righteousness from our souls, or the imposition of the clouds of transgression, that makes it so dark a night in the souls of men. And then there is nothing but enmity and desperate wickedness in the heart of man, and this keeps the stronghold of the affections.[2] There cannot be a further elongation or separation of the soul from God, than to turn so opposite, in all inclinations and dispositions, to his holy will; for the distance between God and us is not local in the point of place; for whither shall we go from him who is everywhere? And thus he is near hand every one of us; but it is also real in the deformity and repugnancy of our natures to his holy will. But add unto this, that being thus separated in affection, and disjoined, as it were, in natural dispositions, we cannot draw near to God in any ordinance—as the Word, prayer, etc. Though we may, as that people, draw near with our lips, and ask of him our duty, and seem to delight to know him, yet there is this natural incapacity and crookedness in the heart of man, that it cannot truly approach unto the Father of spirits with any soul-desire and delight. But their hearts are removed "far from me."[3] I think men might observe that their souls act not in religious business as they should, but that they remove their souls many miles distant from their bodies—and they cannot keep any constancy in this approach

---

1 Ephesians 4:18.
2 Romans 8:7; Jeremiah 17:9.
3 Isaiah 29:13; Matthew 15:8.

of prayer to God, cannot walk with him in their conversation, or carry him along in their meditation. But there is one point of estrangement and separation superadded to all, that there is no man can come near to God without an oblation and offering of peace; that there is no approaching to him, but as to a consuming fire, except we can bring a sacrifice to appease, and a present to please Him for our infinite offenses. There the difference stands—we cannot draw near to walk together, till we be agreed. And, truly, this unto man is impossible, for we have nothing so precious as the redemption of our souls—nothing can compense infinite wrongs, or satisfy infinite justice. Now, this seems to make our nearness again desperate, and to put men furthest off from hope.

Notwithstanding, this is the very purpose of the gospel, preached from the beginning of the world, to remove that distance, and to take impediments of meeting out of the way; for that great obstruction, the want of a sacrifice and ransom, the Lord has supplied it, he himself has furnished it; and it was the great design carried on from the beginning of the world. But as the sun, the nearer he is, the more the earth is enlightened: so here, first some dawning of light appears, as a messenger of hope, to tell that the Redeemer shall come—that the true sacrifice shall be slain; then still the nearer his own appearing, the clearer are the manifestations of him, and the great design is more opened up, till at length he breaks out in glory from under a cloud, and shows himself to the world, to be that Lamb of God that should take away the sins of the world. And now, as the apostle to the Hebrews speaks, "The law has made nothing perfect, but the bringing in of a better hope did, by the which we draw nigh to God."[1] All the sacrifices and shadows that were under the law did but point at this perfect

---

1 Hebrews 7:19.

ransom; and the way of access to God through a Mediator was not so clear; but now the matter is made as hopeful as is possible—the partition-wall of the law's curses—the hand-writing against us is removed on the cross—the enmity slain—the distance removed by the blood of the cross, being partly filled up by his descent into our nature, partly by his lower descent in our nature to suffer death. And this is the savory oblation that we have to present to God, and may have boldness to come nigh because of it. And when once our access is made by the blood of Jesus Christ, then we are called and allowed to come still nigher, to cleave and adhere to him as our Father, to pray unto him, to walk with him. Then we should converse as friends and familiars together; then draw nigh to his light for illumination, and to him as the fountain of life for quickening, to place our delight and desire in him—to forsake all other things, even our wills and pleasures, and to lose them, that they may be found in his; to converse much in his company, and be often in communication with him, and meditation upon him. This is the very design and substance of the gospel. It holds forth the way of making up the breach between man and God, of bringing you nigh who are yet afar off, and nearer who are near hand. O let us hearken to it!

Sermon 6

THE HAPPINESS OF DRAWING NEAR TO GOD

by Thomas Watson

But it is good for me to draw near to God.—Psalm 73:28.

This psalm is no less elegant than sacred; it is calculated for the meridian of God's church in all times; but it is especially fit for the godly to meditate upon in times of calamity. It is entitled a *psalm of Asaph*. Asaph was a man divinely inspired, a prophet; as well as one of the masters of music: It is called a *psalm of Asaph*, either because he composed it, or because it was committed to him to sing. This holy man seems here to have a dialogue with himself concerning providence. He was ready to call God's providences to the bar of reason, and enquire the equity of them. How does it seem just, that those who are evil should enjoy so much good; and those who are good should endure so much evil? While Asaph was debating the case with himself, at last his faith got above his sense; he considered that the wicked were set *in locis lubricis, in slippery places*. And like such as go upon the ice, their feet would soon slide; or like such as walk on mines of powder, they would soon be blown up, verse 18. This did both resolve his doubt, and compose his spirit.

The prœamium or entrance into the psalm is not to be

forgotten, "Truly God is good to Israel"; so the Hebrew renders it *certainly*. Without dispute, this is a golden maxim that must be held. In the Septuagint it is *vox admirantis*, it is set out by way of admiration, *O how good is God to Israel!* What angel in Heaven can express; the vulgar[1] reads it, *veruntanem, yet God is good*; as if the Psalmist had said, though the candle of prosperity shines on the wicked, they have not only what their hearts can wish, but "more than their hearts can wish," verse 7. And though the godly are sorely afflicted, mingling their drink with weeping; yet for all this, "God is good to Israel." Here is the fountain, the stream, the cistern: the fountain is God; the stream, goodness; the cistern into which it runs, Israel. Indeed, God is good "to all."[2] The sweet dew falls upon the thistle as well as the rose. But though God be good *to all*, yet not *alike* good to all. He is good to Israel in a special manner. The wicked have *sparing* mercy, but the godly have saving mercy. And if God be good to his people, then it is good for his people to draw near to him. So it is in the text, "It is good for me to draw near to God."

1. We may look upon the words in *Hypothesi*. Here is something implied, *viz*., that by nature we are far from God.—*Drawing near* implies a strangeness and distance. In our lapsed estate we lost two things, the image of God, and communion with God, "The wicked are estranged from the womb."[3] Every step a sinner takes, is going further from God.—The prodigal's going into a "far country,"[4] was an emblem of the sinner's going afar off from God. How far are they distant from God, who have been traveling forty or fifty years from their

---

1 Vulgar—Common; used by all classes of people; as the vulgar version of the scriptures.—*Webster's 1828 Dictionary.*
2 Psalm 145:9.
3 Psalm 58:3.
4 Luke 15:13.

father's house! and which is worse, sinners are not only far from God, but they do not desire to be near him, "They have loved to wander."[1] Sin does not care to be near holiness. The wicked get as far as they can from God, like Cain, who "went out from the presence of the Lord."[2] That is, the church of God, where were the visible signs of God's presence: he estranged himself from God as much as he could: he *fell to building*, thereby thinking to drown the noise of his conscience, as the Italians of old were wont to drown the noise of thunder by ringing their bells. Sinners think God's company may be best spared, "Cause the Holy One of Israel to cease from before us."[3] Let us shut God out of our company; let him be no more named among us. A bad eye loves not to be near the sun.

Let us be deeply humbled for our fall in Adam, which has set us at such a distance from the blessed God. Heaven and earth are not so far asunder as God and the sinner. The further we are from God, the nearer we are to hell. The further a man sails from the east, the nearer he is to the west. Let us think of returning to God by repentance. Say as the church, "I will go and return to my first husband, for then was it better with me than now."[4]

2. Let us consider the text in Thesi; "It is good for me to draw near to God."

The text falls into these parts. 1. The person, me. 2. The act, draw near. 3. The object, God. 4. The excellency of the act, it is good.

The proposition is this: That it is a great duty incumbent upon Christians to draw near to God, "Let us draw near with a true heart."[5] For the illustration of the proposition, four things

1 Jeremiah 4:9.
2 Genesis 4:16.
3 Isaiah 30:11.
4 Hosea 2:7.
5 Hebrews 10:22.

are to be inquired into.

1. How we are capable of drawing near to God.
2. Where we draw near to God.
3. The manner of our drawing near to God.
4. Why we must draw near to God.

1. How we are capable of drawing near to God. By nature we stand in opposition to God, alienated and enemies.[1] How then can we approach nigh to God?—Answer. It is through a mediator. But Jesus Christ is the screen between us and divine justice. Christ as our High Priest assumes our flesh. Christ's flesh is called a "veil."[2] As Moses when his face shone so exceedingly bright, put a veil upon it, and then Israel might approach near to him and look upon him: so Christ having veiled himself with our human nature, we may now draw near to God and behold him.

And as Christ makes way for us into the Holy of Holies by his incarnation; so by his crucifixion, he died to make God and us friends. The divine law being infringed, God's justice was provoked, and satisfaction demanded, before we could approach to God in an amicable way. Now here Christ as our Priest shed his blood for our sins, and so made the atonement, "Having made peace through the blood of his cross."[3] As Joseph being so great at court, made way for all his brethren to draw near into the king's presence,[4] so Jesus Christ is our Joseph, that makes way for us by his blood, that we may now come near into God's presence. Through Christ, God is pleased with us; he holds forth the golden scepter, that we may draw near, and touch the top of the scepter.

---

1 Colossians 1:21.
2 Hebrews 10:20.
3 Colossians 1:20.
4 Genesis 47:2.

2. Where we draw near to God.

ANSWER. In the use of his ordinances. In the Word we draw near to his Holy Oracle; in the sacrament we draw near to his table. In the one we hear his voice; in the other we have his kiss. Besides, we do in a special manner draw near to God in prayer. Prayer is the soul's private converse and intercourse with God. Prayer whispers in God's ears, "My prayer came before him, even into his ears."[1] In prayer we draw so near to God that we "take hold of him."[2] God draws near to us by his Spirit, and we draw near to him in prayer.

3. The *modus*, or manner of our drawing near to God. God's special residence is in Heaven and we draw near to God, not by the feet of our bodies, but with our souls. The affections are the feet of the soul; by these we move towards God. David drew nigh to God in his desires, "There is none upon earth that I desire beside thee."[3] He did shoot his heart into Heaven by pious ejaculations. Spirits may have intercourse at a distance.

4. Why we must draw near to God.

ANSWER. Because he is our maker, "in him we live." He has given us our bodies; they are his curious "needlework."[4] And as he has wrought the cabinet, so he has put the jewel in it, the precious soul; and surely if we have our being from him, we cannot breathe without him: there is good reason we should draw near to Him in a way of homage and observance.

God is our benefactor; he crowns us with a variety of blessings; he gives health and estate; every bite of bread we eat is reached to us by the hand of Divine bounty. Is there not great

---

1 Psalm 18:6.
2 Isaiah 64:7.
3 Psalm 73:25.
4 Psalm 139:15.

reason we should draw near to him who feeds us? Give a beast provender and he will follow you all the field over. Not to draw near to Him who is our benefactor, is worse than brutish.

God is the *summum bonum*, the chief good. There's enough in God to satisfy the immense desire of the angels. He is *omnimode dulcis*, the quintessence of sweetness; in him all perfections are centered, wisdom, holiness, goodness: he has rivers of pleasure where the soul shall bathe itself forever with infinite delight.[1] So that here is ground sufficient for our drawing near to God; he is the chief good. Everything desires to approach to its happiness.

1. See the right genius and temper of a gracious soul; it is ever drawing near to God; it loves to converse with him in private. A person truly regenerate is not able to stay away long from God, "My soul follows hard after God."[2] A pious soul cannot but draw near to God.

Out of the entire love which he bears to God. It is the nature of love to draw the heart to the object loved.

He who loves his friend will often give him a visit; he that loves God will visit him. The heart ascends to God in a "fiery chariot" of love.

A gracious soul cannot but draw near to God, because of the intimate relationship between God and him. God is a father, "Doubtless you are our father."[3] Does not the child delight to draw near to his father? No father like to God for love; his children shall never want; he has land enough to give to all his heirs. He loves his children so entirely, that he will never disinherit them. How then can believers keep away from their father? they know not how to be long out of his presence.

---

1 Psalm 36.
2 Psalm 63:8.
3 Isaiah 63:16.

A gracious soul cannot choose but draw near to God, because he has found so much sweetness and content in it. While he has drawn near to God, he has drawn virtue from him. Never did Jonathan taste so much sweetness when he dipped his rod in the honey-comb,[1] as the soul finds in communion with God. In drawing near to God a Christian's heart has been warmed and melted; the Lord has kindled his sacrifice from Heaven. In his approaches to God, he has had the illapses[2] of the Spirit, the incomes of God's love, the prelibations[3] of glory: God has given him a "bunch of grapes" by the way; he has "tasted that the Lord is good"; no wonder then he is so frequent in his approaches to the divine majesty; he has found the comfort of drawing near to God.

2. It reproves them, who instead of drawing near to God, draw near to the world. The world engrosses all their time and thoughts, "Who mind earthly things."[4] A good Christian uses the world for his necessity, but his main work is to draw near to God. Whoever he compounds with, and pays short, he will be sure God shall not be a loser. He gives God a daily sacrifice; "he follows God fully."[5] But covetous people make the world their treasure, and what is their treasure, that does most command their hearts. Worldlings live by sense; and to talk to them of drawing nigh to God is to speak riddles and paradoxes to them. They can no more live out of the earth, than the fish out of the water. They have the serpent's curse upon them, "to lick the dust." Things of a worldly aspect draw away the

---

[1] 1 Samuel 14:27.
[2] Illapse—A sliding in; an immission or entrance of one thing into another.—*Webster's 1828 Dictionary.*
[3] Prelibation—Foretaste; a tasting beforehand or by anticipation.—*Webster's 1828 Dictionary.*
[4] Philippians 3:19.
[5] Numbers 14:24.

heart from God. They are *retinacula spei* (as Tertullian says) they hinder our passage to the holy land. Had not the fall beat off men's head-piece of wisdom, they would think thus with themselves, if there be any beauty in the world, what is there in God who made it? He gives the flower its color and odor; he gives the diamond its luster; he gives food its taste; and if there be such sweetness in creatures, what is there in God? He is infinitely better than all. Shall these poor things draw our hearts away from God? shall the drop draw us from the fountain? shall the light of the taper draw us from the sun? shall we admire the gift, and forget the giver? Solomon speaks of a generation of men, "madness is in their heart."[1] Sure they who draw near the world, and leave God, "madness is in their heart." O how empty and insignificant are all other things without God! They are in their matter earthly, in their procuring painful, in their fruition surfeiting, in their duration dying, in their operation damning.

3. It reproves them who draw near to God, but it is hypocritically; they draw nigh with their *lips*, but not with their *hearts*.[2] The Jews (says one) use great shows of adoration, and in their synagogues burn lamps to the honor of God, but no inward devotion can be perceived. What is pomp without piety? Sinners give God the worship of their bodies, but keep their hearts for something else they love better. The heart is a virgin that God himself is suitor to. "My son, give me your heart."[3] To draw near to God with the body, but not the heart is to abuse God. It is as if one should come into an apothecary's shop and ask for cordial water, and he should give him an empty glass. To draw nigh to God without a heart is to play a

---

1 Ecclesiastes 9:3.
2 Isaiah 29:13.
3 Proverbs 23:26.

devotion, and to go to hell covered with religion's mantle.

4. It reproves them who instead of drawing near to God, draw back from God; these are renegades; they once seemed to put forth fair blossoms and gave good hope of their conversion; but their spring is changed to autumn. Either fear of persecution or hope of preferment has turned them away from the profession of religion. Such were Bolsecus, Petrus Carolus, and others. "Israel has cast off the thing that is good."[1] At Ausborough the papists gave ten florins a year to such as revolt from the Protestant faith. Men draw back from God because they never had the Spirit of God to confirm them. Such as have the Spirit's indwelling never take their final leave of God. The Spirit in the heart is called an *earnest*, not a *pawn*. A pawn may be called for again, and taken away, but an earnest remains and is part of the sum behind. O how odious is it to draw back from God! The name Judas is had in abomination at this day. Sure no Protestant would baptize his child, Judas. And how dismal was his end! He who had no bowels to an innocent Christ, his bowels gushed out. If it be good to draw near to God, it must needs be evil to draw back from Him. "Thou hast destroyed all those who go a whoring from thee."[2]

5. It exhorts us all to draw near to God. It is more ingenious to draw near to God voluntarily than to be drawn near to him by affliction. God is the *terminus ad quem;* whither should the soul go but to God? where can the bee rest but in its hive? To draw near to God is both a *privilege* as a *duty*. There are but two motives I shall use to persuade you to this drawing near to God.

1. The first is in the text; to draw near to God is a good thing. "It is good for me." That it is good appears in several ways.

To draw near to God, is our wisdom. "The price of wisdom

---

1 Hosea 8:3.
2 Psalm 73:27.

is above rubies."¹ No jewel we wear does so much adorn us as wisdom; and wherein is our wisdom seen more than in our appropinquation² to God? It is judged wisdom to keep in with great men, "Many will entreat the favor of the Prince."³ A prince's love is mutable. How often does the sunshine of his royal favor set in a cloud. But it is wisdom to draw near to God; he is the sweetest friend, and the sorest enemy.

To draw near to God is our honor. It is counted an honor to converse with noble personages. What high dignity is it, that the great God will allow sinful dust to draw near to him! Surely the apostle did speak of it with an holy boasting, "Our fellowship is with the Father, and with his Son Jesus."⁴ As if he had said, we do not walk with pedantics of the world; we are of the blood-royal of Heaven; we live above other men; "our fellowship is with the Father." That the King of Kings will hold forth a *golden scepter* to us, invite and welcome us into his presence, and bid us draw near; this is no small favor. "Every one that was distressed and in debt, drew near to David, and he became a captain over them."⁵ So that we who are distressed and in debt, may draw near to God; and that he will not *only be our captain*, but our *husband*.⁶ What transcendent dignity is this! It is a wonder God does not kick us out of his presence; but that we should be admitted to see the king's face and that he should send us dainties from his own table, is an honor more fit for angels than men.

To draw near to God is our safety. God is a "strong tower."⁷

---

1 Job 28:18.
2 Appropinquation—a drawing nigh, approach.—*Webster's 1913 Dictionary.*
3 Proverbs 19:6.
4 1 John 1:3.
5 1 Samuel 22:2.
6 Isaiah 54:5.
7 Proverbs 18:10.

It is good in times of danger to draw near to a fort or castle. "He had horns coming out of his hands, and there was the hiding of his power."[1] The horns coming out of God's hands, are to punish his enemies, and the hiding of his power is to safeguard his people. God is an impregnable stronghold. Indeed there is no safety, but in drawing nigh to God. If the sheep straggles from the fold, it is in danger of the wolf; if we straggle and wander from God, we are in danger of Satan.

To draw near to God is our peace. The only thing which breaks our peace is, when we do not keep close to God: but what harmony, yea Heaven is in the soul when it draws nigh to God! "Great peace have they which love your law."[2] This peace, like pearl in broth, is cordial. David drew near to God, for he was "ever with him."[3] And this made his pillow soft when he went to sleep, "I will lay me down in peace";[4] as the honey-dew falls upon the leaf: O that sweet serenity which drops as honey upon the soul, while it is drawing nigh to God! How comfortable it is to draw near to the sun! and how sweet is it to approach nigh to the Sun of Righteousness.

To draw near to God is our riches. It is good drawing near to a gold mine. If we draw near to God, he will enrich us with promises, and divine consolations; he will enrich us with the "pearl of great price." He will reward us as a king, yes as a God.[5] He will make over his land and jewels to us; he will give us the spring flowers of joy here, and the harvest of glory hereafter.

If we draw near to God, he will draw near to us. If we draw near to him in duty, he will draw near to us in mercy.

---

[1] Habakkuk 3:4.
[2] Psalm 119:165.
[3] Psalm 139:18.
[4] Psalm 4:8.
[5] Ephesians 3:8.

When the prodigal approached to his father, his father drew near to him, and fell on his neck, and kissed him.[1] If we draw near to God with repenting hearts, he will draw near to us with a compassionate heart. David prayed, "Draw nigh unto my soul."[2] It is good to have God draw nigh to us. How sweet is his presence! he is light to the eye and joy to the heart. How happy was it for Zaccheus, when Christ drew near to him! "This day is salvation come thy house."[3] When God draws near to the soul, Heaven and salvation draw near.

2. There is a time coming, when we shall wish we had drawn near to God. We are shortly drawing near to our grave, "They draw near unto the gates of death."[4] The wicked who care not for God, yet at death they would desire to draw near to him. Then they cry as "Lord, save or we perish";[5] then mercy, mercy. They run to God in distress, as in a storm men run to a tree for shelter. But God will not shelter his enemies. The Lord gives the sinner abundance of mercy in his lifetime, (as you have seen a loving father bribing a prodigal son with money to see if he can reclaim him) but if the sinner be not wrought upon with mercy, then at death the sun of mercy sets, and a dark night of wrath overtakes the sinner. They who would not draw nigh to God as a friend, will experience that God will draw nigh to them as an enemy.

How shall we do to draw near to God?

Let us contemplate the excellencies of God. He is the "God of glory,"[6] full of orient beauty: in comparison of whom both angels and men are but as the "small dust of the balance."

1 Luke 15:20.
2 Psalm 69:18.
3 Luke 19:9.
4 Psalm 107:18.
5 Matthew 8:25.
6 Psalm 29:3.

He is the "God of love,"[1] who triumphs in acts of mercy. Well may this encourage us in our approaches to him who delights to display the banner of free grace to sinners. If we should hear of a person of honor, who was of a lovely disposition, obliging all that came to him by acts of kindness and civility, it would make us ambitiously desirous to ingratiate ourselves with him and to obtain his acquaintance. God is the most sovereign good, the wonder of love, ready to diffuse the silver streams of his bounty to indigent creatures; this, if any thing, will make us willing to draw near to him and acquiesce in him as the center of felicity.

If we would draw near to God, let us study our own wants. Let us consider in what need we stand of God, and that we cannot be happy without him. The prodigal never drew near to his father, until he "began to be in want."[2] A proud sinner, who was never convinced of his want, minds not to come near God; he has a stock of his own to live upon, "We are lords; we will come no more unto thee."[3] A full stomach despises the honey-comb. It is the sense of need which brings us near to God. Why did so many lame and paralytics resort to Christ, but because they wanted a cure. Why does the thirsty man draw near to a fountain, but because he wants water. Why does a condemned man draw near his prince, but because he wants a pardon. When a poor soul reviews its wants, I want grace; I want the favor of God, I am damned without Christ; this makes him draw near to God, and be an earnest supplicant for mercy.

If we would draw near to God, let us be careful to clear our interest in God, "Let us draw near with a true heart in full

---

1 2 Corinthians 13:11.
2 Luke 15:14.
3 Jeremiah 2:31.

assurance of faith."[1] When we know him to be our God, then we draw near to him. The spouse, by virtue of the conjugal union, draws near to her husband, "This God is our God."[2]

Let us beg the Holy Spirit. The Spirit of God has a magnetic virtue. Corruption draws the heart from God; the Spirit draws it to him, "Draw me, we will run after thee."[3] The Spirit, by his omnipotent grace, draws the heart to God not only sweetly, but powerfully.

Let us get our hearts fired with love to God: which way the love goes, that way the heart is drawn. If God be the treasure delighted in, our hearts will be drawn to him. Servile fear makes the soul fly from God; sacred love makes it fly to him.

---

1 Hebrews 10:22.
2 Psalm 48:14.
3 Song of Solomon 1:4.

Sermon 7

THE SAINT'S HAPPINESS

By Richard Sibbes

But it is good for me to draw near to God.—PSALM 73:28.

This psalm is a psalm of Asaph, or of David, commended to Asaph, who was a seer and a singer. It represents one in a conflict afterward recovered, and in a triumphant conclusion. It begins abruptly, as if he had gained this truth: Say flesh and Satan what they can, yet this I am resolved of, I find God is yet good to Israel. Then he discovers what was the cause of this conflict. It was his weakness and doubt of God's promises in verse 13, occasioned from the great prosperity that the wicked enjoyed, described from the 2ND verse to the 13TH. Then he sets down his recovery in the 17TH verse. He went into the sanctuary, and saw what God meant to do with them at last. Then follows the accomplishment of the victory in the 23RD verse. I am continually with thee. Thou has holden me up. Thou will guide me now and bring me to glory. Therefore there is none in heaven but thee. Though nature may be surprised, yet God is my help; and for the wicked, they shall perish; nay, thou has destroyed them. Therefore "it is good for me to draw nigh to God."

Now from that which has been laid open we may observe,

DOCTRINE. First, *That God's dearest children are exercised with sharp conflicts in the faith of principles, yea, of God's providence.* This should comfort such as God suffers to cast forth mire and dirt of incredulity. It is the common case of God's dearest children, yea, of the prophets of God, David, Jeremiah, and Habakkuk, and therefore we ought not to be dejected too much; and the rather because—which also we may note in the second place—

DOCTRINE. Second, *God's children, though they be thus low, yet they shall recover,* and after recovery comes a triumph. They may begin to slip a little, but still God's hand is under them, and his goodness ever lower than they can fall; and this should teach us to discern of our estates aright, and to expect such conflicts, yet to know that still God's Spirit will not be wanting to check and repress such thoughts in the fittest time. Contrarily it is a principle to wicked men to doubt of God's providence, and therefore they suffer such temptations to rule in them.

In the next place observe,

DOCTRINE. Third, *The way for a Christian to recover his ground in time of temptation, is for him to enter into God's sanctuary,* and not to give liberty to his thoughts to range in, considering the present estate that he is in; but look to former experiences, in himself, in others; see the promises and apply them; it shall go well with the righteous, but woe to the wicked, it shall not go well with them. This is to go into the sanctuary; and happy man you are, and in high favor, whom God admits so near to him. The world will tell you of corn, and wine, and oil, and how great and glorious men are here; but the sanctuary will show you they are set in slippery places. Carnal reason will tell you God has left the earth; he sees not, he governs not, all are out of order. But the sanctuary will show you all things are beautiful in their time.[1] Mark the end of the righteous.[2] See Joseph, once a prisoner, after lord of Egypt; Lazarus, once contemned and despised, after in Abraham's bosom; Christ himself, once a rebuke and scorn of all on the cross, but now triumphing on "the right hand of God, far above all principalities and power."[3] All God's ways are mercy and truth, though we seem never so much forsaken for the present. Again, from David's observing the state of wicked men—it is said, he saw the prosperity of wicked men—we may gather,

DOCTRINE. Fourth, *Whether it be the eye of faith or the eye of sense, all serves to bring us nearer to God.* God represents to the outward view of his children the example of his justice on others, to draw his children nearer home; and it is one main reason why God suffers variety of conditions in men, that his children may gain experience from seeing their behavior and by conversing with them.

Last of all, from the connection of this text with the former words, observe,

DOCTRINE. Fifth, *That the course of the children of God is a course contrary to the stream of the world.* "They withdraw away from thee, and shall perish," saith the prophet, but "it is good for me to draw near"; as if he had said, Let others take what course they will, it matters not much, I will look to myself, "it is good for me to draw near to God"; and the reason is,

REASON 1. *Because they are guided by the Spirit of God*, which is contrary to the world, and the Spirit teaches them to see, not after the opinions of the world that is their best friend, but God is my best friend, that will never forsake me. "Many walk that are enemies to the cross of Christ, but our

---

1 Ecclesiastes 3:11.
2 Psalm 37:37.
3 Ephesians 1:21.

conversation is in heaven."[1] And then a Christian has experience of the ways of God, and by it he is every day settled in them; by it he sees what the world works in others, and how God is opposite to them, and thereby he is made more zealous; as in winter time the body is more hot within than in summer. And those that are well grounded grow more strong by opposition; and however they may sometimes stagger, yet their motion is constant.

Use. If we will know our estates, *examine after what rule we lead our life, and what principles we follow*. If outward weights of the love of the world, self-love, or the like do move us, as clocks that go no longer than the weights hang on them, this shows that we are but actors of the life of a Christian, and that we are not naturally moved, that our nature is not changed, and that we are not made "partakers of the divine nature,"[2] for then our motion would come from above: "My life and flesh may fail, but thou, Lord, wilt never fail."[3] Therefore it is good for me to draw near to thee; which words proceeding from an experimental trial of David, of the goodness and happiness of this nearness to God, afford us this consideration,

Doctrine. Sixth, *That God's Spirit enables his children by experience to justify wisdom*. He suffers his children to meet with oppositions, that they may see they stand by an almighty power above their own, and above the power of their enemies. *Nihil tam certum est, quam quod post dubium certum est*, and therefore those that have felt the bitterness of their sins know how bitter it is; and those that have been overcome in temptations know their nature is weak, and those that have felt the unconstancy of the world, and the vanity of it, know it is

---

1 Philippians 3:20.
2 2 Peter 1:4.
3 Psalm 40:12.

a bitter thing to be far from God, and therefore they resolve, "I will go to my first husband; for then it was better with me than now";[1] and as the prodigal, "There is meat enough in my father's house, why then do I perish here with hunger?"[2] and therefore, if we will ever think to stand out resolutely in our courses against trials, we must labor for experience, and diligently observe God's dealings. It is experience that breeds patience and hope. Experience of a truth seals a truth with a *probatum est*. And without it, the best and strongest judgments will in time of trial be ready to be jostled out of the maintenance thereof, and great professors will be ashamed of their good courses.

But to come to the particulars. "It is good"; that is, it puts in us a blessed quality and disposition. It makes a man to be like God himself; and, secondly, "it is good," that is, it is comfortable; for it is the happiness of the creature to be near the Creator; it is beneficial and helpful.

"To draw near." How can a man but be near to God, seeing he fills heaven and earth: "Whither shall I go from thy presence?"[3] He is present always in power and providence in all places, but graciously present with some by his Spirit, supporting, comforting, strengthening the heart of a good man. As the soul is said to be *tota in toto*, in several parts by several faculties, so God, present he is to all, but in a diverse manner. Now we are said to be near to God in divers degrees: *First*, when our *understanding is enlightened; intellectus est veritatis sponsa;* and so the young man speaking discreetly in things concerning God, is said not to be far from the kingdom of God.[4]

---

1 Hosea 2:7.
2 Luke 15:17.
3 Psalm 139:7.
4 Mark 12:34.

Secondly, in minding; when God is present to our minds, so as the soul is said to be present to that which it mindeth; contrarily it is said of the wicked, that "God is not in all their thoughts."[1] *Thirdly*, when the *will upon the discovery of the understanding comes to choose the better part, and is drawn from that choice to cleave to him*, as it was said of Jonathan's heart, "it was knit to David."[2] *Fourthly*, when *our whole affections are carried to God*, loving him as the chief good. Love is the first-born affection. That breeds desire of communion with God. Thence comes joy in him, so as the soul pants after God, "as the hart after the water springs."[3] *Fifthly*, and especially, *when the soul is touched with the Spirit of God working faith*, stirring up dependence, confidence, and trust on God. Hence arises sweet communion. The soul is never at rest till it rests on him. Then it is afraid to break with him or to displease him. But it grows zealous and resolute, and hot in love, stiff in good cases; resolute against his enemies. And yet this is not all, for God will have also the outward man, so as the whole man must present itself before God in word, in sacraments; speak of him and to him with reverence, and yet with strength of affection mounting up in prayer, as in a fiery chariot; hear him speak to us; consulting with his oracles; fetching comforts against distresses, directions against maladies. *Sixthly*, and especially, we draw near to him *when we praise him;* for this is the work of the souls departed, and of the angels in heaven, that are continually near unto him. And thus much for the opening of the words. The prophet here says, "It is good for me." How came he to know this? Why, he had found it by experience, and by it he was thoroughly convinced of it; so

---

1 Psalm 10:4.
2 1 Samuel 18:1.
3 Psalm 42:1.

DOCTRINE. Seventh, *Spiritual conviction is the ground of practice;* for naturally the will follows the guidance of the understanding; and when it is convicted[1] of the goodness of this or that thing, the will move toward it. Now there are four things that go to conviction: *first,* the understanding must be enlightened to see the truth of the thing, that there is such a thing, and that it is no fancy; *secondly,* we must know it to be good, as the gospel is called the good word of God; *thirdly,* that it is good for me; and *lastly,* upon comparing all these together, it is the best for me of all, though other things seem to be good in their kind. A wicked man may be convinced that heaven and grace are good things; but his corrupted affections persuade him it is better to live in pleasure and lust; and when death comes then he may repent, for God is merciful. But a good man prefers drawing near to God above all, and therefore we should labor for this conviction of our spirits. For it is not enough to hear, read, discourse, pray, but we must get the Spirit to set to his seal to all upon our hearts; and this made Moses in sober balancing of things, choose rather to draw near to God and join with his afflicted brethren, than to be in honor in Pharaoh's court, to be the son of Pharaoh's daughter, or to enjoy the pleasures of sin, "for he had respect to the reward."[2] He was convinced that there was more to be gotten with them than amongst the Egyptians. Thus Abraham came to forsake his country, and the disciples to forsake all and follow Christ. And undoubtedly the ground of all profaneness is from atheism that is within. Would the swearer trample upon the name of God, if he did believe and were convinced that he should not be guiltless? Would the filthy person come near strange flesh, if he were persuaded that God would judge? Would any

---
1 That is, "convinced."—G.
2 Hebrews 11:26.

wicked man change an eternal joy for a minute's pleasure, if he did believe the unrighteous should not inherit the kingdom of God? Nay, the best have a remainder of this corruption of atheism. David: "So foolish was I, and a beast."[1] From hence come all sin against knowledge and conscience in men, whereof David complains: "Keep me, that presumptuous sins prevail not over me, or get not dominion over me."[2] And for remedy against this vile corruption, there is no way but the immediate help of the Holy Spirit; and therefore, it is said that the Spirit, when it comes, "shall convince the world of sin";[3] that is, it shall so manifest sin to be in the whole world, because of the general unbelief, as they shall see no remedy but in Christ; and therefore we should beforehand search out the crafty allurements to sin, that we may be provided to give them an answer when they set upon us, lest we be suddenly overcome, and labor to see the excellency of the things that are freely given us of God, which amongst other titles are called a feast, "a feast of fat things."[4] Now if we will not feast with him, how do we ever think to suffer with him if he should call us thereto? "It is good." How is it good? Both in quality and condition; for while we are here in this world we are strangers, and in an estate of imperfection as it were. Paul says, while he was present in the body he was absent from the Lord; and the more near perfection we are, the more near must we be to the ground of all perfection, and this is only in God. For, *first, he is goodness itself.* He has the beauty of all, the strength of all, the goodness of all, originally in himself. He is the gathering together of all excellency and goodness. *Secondly,* he is *the universal good.* He is good to all.

---

1 Psalm 73:22.
2 Psalm 19:13.
3 John 16:8.
4 Isaiah 25:6.

What all has that is good, comes from him. Of creatures, some have beauty, others riches, others have honors, but God has all together. *Thirdly,* he is *the all-sufficient and satisfactory good.* The goodness of no creature can give full content; for the soul of man is capable of more than all created goodness together can satisfy. Only it is filled with God's likeness, and satisfied with communion with him. The best thing here to satisfy the soul, as Solomon witnesseth, is knowledge; and yet it contents not the heart of man: *sine Deo omnis copia est egestas,* [says] Bernard.[1] God alone fills every corner of the soul in him. We are swallowed up with "joy unspeakable," and "peace that passes understanding." "Eye cannot see it, ear cannot hear it, heart of man cannot conceive those things which even in this life are but beams of his brightness."[2] *Fourthly,* God is a goodness *that is proportionable and fitting to our souls,* which is the best part in a man; and that which we draw near unto must communicate some loveliness, for that moves us to draw near to it. Now God is a Spirit fit to converse with our spirits; and he is love, and can answer the love and drawing near of our spirits with love and drawing near to us again. The things of this world cannot love us so as to give us content, or to help us in the day of wrath. *Fifthly, nothing can make us happy but drawing near to God.* If there were nothing in the world better than man, then man would be content with himself; but by nature it is evident man sees a better happiness than is in himself, and therefore he seeks for it out of himself. And as Solomon tried all things, and found no happiness but in the fear of God, so man cannot rest in any outward content till he comes to God as the Creator of all happiness, and the spring-head from whence the soul had its original; and therefore, "All

---

1 A frequent sentiment in his Letters.—G.
2 1 Corinthians 2:9.

the gospel is to this end, that we may have fellowship with the Father, and his Son Jesus Christ";[1] and "Christ's sufferings [were] to this end, that being dead in flesh, but quickened in the spirit, he might bring us again to God."[2] "That he might gather all into one head."[3] By sin we were scattered from God, from angels, and from our ourselves; but now by Christ we are made one, with one another, and with the holy angels, one with God our chief good.

For use hereof, it *should teach us to labor to attain to this estate of being spiritually convinced of the goodness of God*, that we may by experience say, "It is good for me to draw near to God," for God will not esteem of us according to our knowledge, but as our affections are, and therefore the wicked man he calls a worldling, because the world fills him, let his knowledge be never so great. And the church in the Revelation is called heaven, because their affections and minds are that way,[4] and again, the more we are convinced of God's goodness, the better we are; for God's goodness, tasted and felt by the soul, ennobles it, as a pearl set in a gold ring makes it the more rich and precious. But to come to the estate that is so commended to us, it is described to us by drawing near unto God, so as we may take this for a received ground, that

DOCTRINE. Eighth, *Man's happiness is in communion with God.* Before the fall of man, there was a familiar conversation with God; but by the sin of our first parents we lost this great happiness, and now we are strangers, and as contrary to God as light is contrary to darkness, and hell to heaven; he holy, we impure; he full of knowledge, we stark fools; and instead

---

1 1 John 1:3.
2 1 Peter 3:18.
3 Ephesians 1:10, 22.
4 Revelation 21:1.

of delighting in him, we now tremble at his presence, and are afraid of such creatures as approach nigh to him, trembling at the presence of angels, nay, afraid of a holy man. "What have I to do with thee, thou man of God? art thou come to call my sins to remembrance?"[1] And therefore we fly the company of good men, because their carriage and course of life do upbraid us; and hence it is that at the least apprehension of God's displeasure, wicked men do quake. The heathen emperor trembled at a thunder clap.[2] But God, in his infinite mercy and goodness, left us not, but entertaining a purpose to choose some to draw near unto him; and to this end he has found out a way for man and him to meet, but no way for the angels; and the foundation of this union is in Christ, in whom he reconciled the world to himself; for he being God, became man, so to draw man back again unto God; and thus, like Jacob's ladder, one end of it is in heaven, the other on earth. The angels ascending and descending show a sweet intercourse between God and man, now reconciled together, so as Christ is now "a living way" for ever, being "the way, the truth, and the life." He is a way far more near and sure than we had in Adam; for in him God was in man, but now man subsists in God, so as our nature is now strengthened by him, who also has enriched it and advanced it: and what he has wrought in his own human nature, he by little and little will work in all his mystical members; so being once far off, we are now made near, and this he did principally by his death, for reconciliation is made by his blood,[3] and thus, by the admirable mystery of his deep wisdom, he has found a means to make the seeming opposite attributes of justice and mercy to kiss each other, so as we are

---

1 1 Kings 17:18.
2 This is told of Nero.—G.
3 Colossians 1:20.

saved, and yet his infinite justice has full content. For how could his hatred of sin appear more gloriously than in punishing it upon his own only beloved Son? And therefore worthily he is called "our peace"; for he is that great peacemaker offering himself up, and us in him, "as a sweet-smelling sacrifice, acceptable to God,"[1] being then thus brought near to God, to keep and maintain this nearness, so as nothing may separate us again. He has put into us his own Spirit, so as we are one spirit with Christ; and by that Spirit he works in us and by us by that Spirit. We hear, read, pray, and as by the soul in us our bodies do live, breathe, and move, and the like, so he makes his Spirit to move in us to a holy conversation and a heavenly life, being thus made "partakers of the divine nature,"[2] and this sanctifies us to a holy communion with God; and therefore the apostle prays, "The grace of our Lord Jesus Christ, the love of God the Father, and the communion of the Holy Ghost, be with them";[3] that is, for a fuller manifestation of the love of God in sending Christ, the grace of Christ in coming to us, and the communion of the Holy Spirit, because by it we are made to live a holy life, and to communicate with God; and thus the three persons in Trinity conspire together in reducing man back again to be more near to God.

USE 1. Now, for use of this, it should teach us *how to think on God*, not as all justice and power, hating sin and sinners, but as a Father, now laying aside terrible things that may scare us from drawing nigh to him, and as a God, stooping down to our human nature, to take both it and our miserable condition upon himself, and see our nature not only suffering with Christ, but rising, nay, now in heaven united to God; and this

---

1 Philippians 4:18.
2 2 Peter 1:4.
3 2 Corinthians 13:14.

will feed the soul with inestimable comfort.

Use 2. *Secondly*, Labor to be more near to him, *by the more full participation of his Spirit*. Those that have not Christ's Spirit are none of his. By it we in Christ have access to God; and therefore the more spiritual we are, the nearer access we have to the secrets of God. In our first estate, we are altogether flesh, and have no spirit; in our present estate of grace, we are partly flesh and partly spirit; in our third estate in heaven, we shall be all spiritual; yea, our bodies shall be spiritual.[1] It is sown natural, but it shall be raised spiritual, and shall be obedient to our souls in all things, and our souls wholly possessed and led by the Spirit of God, so as then God shall be all in all with us; and for means hereunto,

First, Labor to be conversant in spiritual means, as in hearing of the Word, receiving of the sacraments. God annexes his Spirit to his own ordinances; and thence it is that in the communion with God in the ordinances, men's apprehensions are so enlarged as they are many times spiritually sick, and do long after the blessed enjoying of God's presence in heaven. But take heed how we come, think what we have to do, and with whom. Come not without the garment of Christ; and it is no matter how beggarly we are, this food is not appointed for angels, but for men. And come with an humble heart, as Elizabeth. "Who am I, that (not the mother of my Lord) God himself from heaven should come to me!"[2]

Secondly, Converse with those that draw near unto him. God is present where two or three are assembled in his name, warming their hearts with love and affection, as it is said of the two disciples going to Emmaus, "Did not our hearts burn within us while we walked in the way, and conferred of the

---
1 1 Corinthians 15:44.
2 Luke 1:43.

sayings?" etc.[1] Oh, it is a notable sign of a spiritual heart to seek spiritual company; for when their hearts join together, they warm one another, and are hereby guarded from temptations; nay, the wicked themselves in God's company will be restrained. Saul, a wicked man, amongst the prophets will prophesy now.[2] If by good company carnal men themselves do in a manner draw near to God, how acceptable ought this to be to us, and how powerful in us.

Thirdly, And especially, *be much in prayer;* for this is not only a main part of this duty of drawing near to God, but it is a great help thereunto. God is near to all that call upon him; for then are those most near to God when their understandings, affections, desires, trust, hope, faith, are busied about God; and therefore as Moses's face did shine with being in the presence of God, so those that are conversant in this duty of prayer have a luster cast upon their souls, and their minds brought into a heavenly temper, and made fit for anything that is divine. I could wish that men would be more in public prayer, and that they would not forget private prayer, if ever they intend the comfort of their souls, not only hereafter, but even during this present life. For every day's necessities and dangers in the midst of many enemies, the devil, flesh, and world, ill company, and strong corruptions, should invite us to cast ourselves into the protection of an almighty Saviour. There is not a minute of time in all our life but we must either be near God or we are undone.

Fourthly, Observe *the first motions of sin in our hearts*, that may "grieve the Spirit of God" in the least manner, and check them at the first. Give no slumber to your eyes, then, nor the reins to your desires: "Thou, O man of God, flee the lusts of

---

1 Luke 24:32.
2 1 Samuel 10:12.

youth."[1] The best things in us, if they come from nature in us, God abhors. Rebuke therefore the first motions, before they come to delight or action. God abhors one that gives liberty to his thoughts, more than one that falls into a grievous sin now and then, through strength of temptation; and such shall find comfort sooner of the pardon of their sins, for they cannot but see their offenses to be heinous, and so have ground of abasement in themselves; but the other, thinking of the smallness of their sins, or at least that God is not much offended with thoughts, do fill themselves with contemplative wickedness, and chase away the Spirit of God, that cannot endure an unclean heart. We must therefore keep ourselves pure and unspotted of this present world, "for the pure in heart shall see God,"[2] and "without holiness none shall ever see him."[3] The least sin in thought, if it be entertained, it eats out the strength of the soul, that it can receive no good from God, nor close with him, so as it performs all duties deadly and hollowly. "If I regard iniquity in my heart, the Lord will not hear my prayer";[4] and hence it is that so little good is wrought in the ordinances of God. Men bring their lusts along with them. They neither know the sweetness of the presence of God's Spirit, neither do they desire it. It is a true rule that every sin has intrinsically in it some punishment; but it is not the punishment that is the proper venom or poison of sin, but this, that it hinders the Spirit of God from us, and keeps us from him, and unfits us for life or for death. But this inward divorce from God's Spirit above all it is the most bitter stab that can befall any one that ever tasted of the sweetness of Christian profession.

---

1 2 Timothy 2:22.
2 Matthew 5:8.
3 Hebrews 12:14.
4 Psalm 66:18.

Now, for the better keeping of our thoughts, we should labor to watch against our outward senses, that by them thoughts be not darted into us. "The eyes of the fool are in the corners of the world,"[1] says the wise man; and therefore let men profess what they will, when they go to lewd company and filthy places, where corruptions are shot into them by all their senses, they neither can take delight to draw near to God, nor can God take any delight to draw near to them. Dinah, that will be straying abroad, comes home with shame; and that soul that either straggles after temptations, or suffers temptations to enter into it uncontrolledly, both ways grieves God, and that good Spirit that should lead us to him. As for such as live in gross sins, as lying, blaspheming, swearing, drunkenness, adultery, or the like, let them never think of drawing near to God. They must first be civilized before they can appear to be religious; and they contrarily proclaim to the whole world that they say to God, "Depart from us, for we will none of thy ways,"[2] so as God draws away from them, and they draw away from him.

Fifthly, Be in God's walks and ordinances in a coarse of doing good, in our Christian or civil calling, sanctified by prayer and a holy dependence upon God for strength, wisdom, and success. Go not out of those ways wherein he gives his angels charge of our persons and actions, and whatever we do. Labor to do it with perfection, as our Father in heaven is perfect.

Sixthly, Observe God's dealings with the church, both formerly and now in these days, and how he deals and has formerly dealt with ourselves, that from experience of his faithfulness to us we may gather confidence to approach nigh him at any occasion. God's works and words do answer one another:

---

1 Proverbs 17:24.
2 Job 21:14.

"Hath he said, and shall he not do it?"[1] He is always good to Israel. Observe therefore how all things work together for your particular drawing nigh unto him; for if all do work together for your good, then it must be of necessity for your drawing near to God, and drawing you away from this present world; and observe how your soul answers the purpose of God, how your affections are bent, and so how all comes out for your benefit at last. See God in afflictions embittering ill courses in you; in your success in your affairs, encouraging you; and thus walk with God. But evermore think of him as of a Father in covenant with you.

Seventhly, Labor to maintain humility, having evermore a sense of your unworthiness, and wants, and continual dependence on God, and thus humble yourself to walk with him. Hence the saints in God's presence call themselves "dust and ashes,"[2] as Abraham, "and less than the least of God's mercies,"[3] as Jacob. God is "a consuming fire,"[4] and will be sanctified in all that come nigh unto him. He will give grace to the humble, but beholds the proud afar off, as they look on others: "Draw near to the Lord, and he will draw near to you."[5] Humble yourselves under "the mighty hand of God," and he will lift you up. He that lifts himself up, makes himself a god; and God will endure no co-rivals. Contrarily, he dwells in the heart of the humble,[6] and in the Psalms, "An humble and a contrite heart, O God, thou wilt not despise." But pride he abhors an abomination of desolation.

Eighthly, Labor for sincerity in all our actions. Whatever we do to God or man, do it with a single eye, resolute to please God.

---

1 Numbers 23:19.
2 Genesis 18:27.
3 Genesis 32:10.
4 Hebrews 12:29.
5 James 4:8.
6 Isaiah 66:2.

Let men say what they will, "a double-minded man is unstable in all his ways,"[1] and what is a double-minded man, but one that has one eye on God, another on a by-respect? If religion fail him, he will have favor of men, or wealth, yet would fain have both, for credit sake. Such are gross temporizers; and in time, of temporizers [it] will appear that their religion serves but for a cloak to their vile hypocrisy. This God loathes, and will "spew them out."[2]

Ninthly, Observe *the first motions of God's Spirit;* and give diligent heed to them, for by these God knocks for entrance into the heart: "Behold, I stand at the door and knock."[3] God is near when he knocks, when he puts inclinations into the heart, and sharpens them with afflictions. If, then, we stop our ears, we may say "the kingdom of God was near unto us"; but if he once ceases knocking, our mouths shall for ever be stopped; and for this reason it is that so many live daily under the means, and yet live in vile courses, as if God had determined their doom. They resisted the first motions, and close with their lusts, and so God pronounces a curse: "Make this people's heart fat."[4] On the contrary, those that will open to God while he continues knocking, God will come in and make an everlasting tabernacle in them, and sup with them.[5]

Lastly, Take up daily controversies that do arise in us, through the inconstancy of our deceivable hearts. Repentance must be every day's work, renewing our covenant, especially every morning and evening; repair breaches by confession; and considering the crossness of our hearts, commit them to God

---

1 James 1:8.
2 Revelation 3:16.
3 Revelation 3:20.
4 Isaiah 6:10.
5 Revelation 3:20.

by prayer: "Knit my heart to thee, that I may fear thy name."[1]

A THIRD USE of this doctrine is of *instruction;* and, *first*, to teach us *that a Christian that thus draws near to God is the wisest man.* He has God's Word, reason, and experience to justify his course. He is the wisest man that is wise for himself. The Christian feels it and knows it, and can justify himself. Paul suffered, and was not ashamed. Why? "I know," saith he, "whom I have believed."[2] Let men scorn, I pass[3] not for man's censure. They shall never scorn me out of my religion; and for them, the Scripture, that can best judge, calls those wicked men fools; for they refuse God, who is the chiefest good, and seek for content where none is to be found. Contrarily, if we do affect honor, or riches, or pleasure, God is so gracious as in religion he gives us abundance of these. In God is all fullness; in Christ are unsearchable riches; in God everlasting strength, "and his favor is better than the life itself."[4] Ahithophel was wise, but it was to hang himself; Saul a mighty man, but to shed his own blood; Haman's honor ended in shame.

Secondly, Hence we may learn *how to justify zeal in religion.* If to be near God be good, then the nearer him the better; if religion be good, then the more the better; if holiness be good, then the more the better; it is best to excel in the best things. Who was the best man but Christ, and why? He was nearest the fountain. And who are next but the angels, and why? Because they are always in God's presence. And who next but those that are nearest to Christ. If we could get angelical holiness, were it not commendable? And therefore it should shame us to be backward, and cold, and to have so little zeal,

---

1 Psalm 86:11.
2 2 Timothy 1:12.
3 That is, "pause"=care for.—G.
4 Psalm 63:3.

as to be ashamed of goodness, as most are.

Thirdly, This should teach us *that a man must not break with God for any creature's sake whatever.* It is good to lose all for God. Why? Because we have riches in him, liberty in him, all in him. A man may be a king on earth, and yet a prisoner in himself; and if we lose anything, though it be our own life, for God, we shall save it. If we be swallowed up of outward misery, the Spirit of God, that "searcheth the deep things of God,"[1] passes and repasses, and puts a relish into us of the "unsearchable riches of Christ."[2] "Taste and see how good God is."[3] "How excellent is thy loving-kindness, which thou have laid up for them that fear thee."[4] "How precious are thy thoughts to me, O Lord."[5] "Thou has the words of everlasting life, whither then shall I go?" said Peter, when he felt but a spark of the divine power.[6]

A FOURTH USE of this doctrine shall be an use of *trial, to know whether we draw near to God or not.*

First, therefore, where this is, there will be *a further desire of increase of communion with God.* The soul will not rest in measure.[7] Moses had divers entertainments of God: he had seen him in "the bush," and in mount Sinai, and many other times; but not contented herewith, he would needs see God's face. And thus Abraham, he gathers upon God still more and more ground in his prayers: "What if fifty, what if forty, what if twenty, what if ten righteous be found there?" says he.[8]

---

1 1 Corinthians 2:10.
2 Ephesians 3:8.
3 Psalm 34:8.
4 Psalm 36:7.
5 Psalm 139:17.
6 John 6:68.
7 Exodus 33:11, seq.
8 Genesis 18:24, seq.

And Jacob, how often was he blessed whom Isaac blessed, when he was to go into Paran! when he was there at his return; and yet when he comes to wrestle with the angel, "I will not let thee go till thou bless me."¹ And the reason is, because as God is a fountain never to be drawn dry, so is man an emptiness never filled, but our desires increase still till we arrive in heaven; and therefore the more we work, and the more we pray, and the more good we do, the more do our desires increase in doing good.

Secondly, This will appear *in abasing or humbling ourselves,* as it was with Abraham. The more near God is, the more humbly he falls on his face, and confesses he is but "dust and ashes." The angels, in token of reverence, do cover their faces, "being in the presence of God." And it is an universal note, that all such as draw near to God, they are humble and reverent in holy duties; and therefore proud persons have no communion with God at all.

Thirdly, The nearer we are to God, the more we admire heavenly things; and count all others "dross and dung," as St. Paul.² When the sun rises, the stars they vanish; and those that do not admire the joy, peace, and happiness of a Christian, are unacquainted with drawing near to God.

Fourthly, When we have a sense and sight of sin, then we may truly be said to "draw near," and to be near to God; for by his light are our eyes enlightened, and we are quickened by his heat and love; and hence we come to see little sins great sins, and are afraid of the beginnings of sin: "Lord, purge me from my secret sins; create in me a new heart; oh let the thoughts of my heart be always acceptable in thy sight."³ And those that

---

1 Genesis 32:26.
2 Philippians 3:8.
3 Psalm 19:14.

make no scruple of worldly affairs on the Lord's Day, of light, small oaths, as they call them, or of corrupt discourse, they neither are nor can draw near to God.

Fifthly, The nearer we draw to God, the more is our rest. "Come unto me, all you that are weary and heavy laden, and you shall find rest unto your souls."[1] "The sorrows of those that worship another god shall be multiplied," and therefore they may well maintain doubting. And therefore such, if they be in their right minds, never end their days comfortably.

Sixthly, In all distresses, those that draw near to God will fly to him with confidence; but a guilty conscience is afraid of God, as of a creditor that owes him punishment, or that intends to cast him into perpetual prison. And as a child will in all his wrongs go and complain to his father,[2] so if we have the spirit of sons we have access to God, and peace with God, and can come boldly to the throne of grace, to find help in him at need.

Seventhly, He that is near to God is neither afraid of God nor of any creature, for God and he are in good terms. In the midst of thundering and lightning, Moses has heart to go near, when the Israelites fly, and stand afar off: "The Lord is the strength of my salvation, of whom shall I be afraid?"[3] "He that feareth the Lord will not be afraid of evil tidings";[4] but, contrarily, on the wicked there are fears, and snares, and pits. They fear where no cause of fear is; and when God reveals his terror, indeed then, "the sinners in Sion are afraid, and the hypocrites that make show of holiness are surprised with fearfulness; who amongst us shall dwell with devouring fire, and who amongst us shall dwell with everlasting burnings?"[5]

---

1 Matthew 11:28; Psalm 16:4.
2 Romans 5:2, seq.
3 Psalm 27:1.
4 Psalm 112:7.
5 Isaiah 33:14.

Eighthly, The nearer we are to God, the more in love we will be with spiritual exercises; the more near to God, the more in love with all means to draw nigh to him; as of books, sermons, good company. My delight "is in the excellent of the earth,"[1] "Oh how I love thy law,"[2] "How beautiful are thy dwelling-places, O Lord of hosts."[3]

Ninthly, He that is near God *is so warmed with love of him, so that he will stand against opposition*, and that out of experience—"He that delivered me out of the paw of the bear, will deliver me from the hands of this uncircumcised Philistine,"[4]—and out of his experience he will be encouraged to use the ordinances of God. He will pray, because he has found the sweetness of it; he will be in good company, because he finds it preserves him in a better temper for the service of God; he will hear the word spiritually and plainly laid open to him, because he has found the power of it in renewing and quickening his affections and desires; and those that do not draw nigh to God, do either loathe, or at least are indifferent, to days, to companies, to exercises. All are alike to them; and they wonder at the niceness of Christians that take so much labor and pains, when as a man may go to heaven at an easier rate by much; and, on the contrary, Christians do as much wonder at them, that they are so careless, when as "few are called"; and of those that are called, some "hear the word, but receive it not." Some receive, "and in time of trial fall off,"[5] so as not the third part of hearers are saved. What then now remains but that we should be *encouraged unto this duty of drawing near unto God*. We see how Scripture, reason, and

1 Psalm 16:3.
2 Psalm 119:97.
3 Psalm 84:1.
4 1 Samuel 17:37.
5 Luke 8:5.

experience proves that it is a thing necessary and profitable; and those that are far from God shall perish, and those that go a-whoring from him he will destroy, as it is in the foregoing verse. Those that are either of a whorish judgment, or affections after lust or covetousness, or the like, God will curse, for all sin is but adultery, or defiling of the soul with the creature; and therefore labor for chaste judgments and affections; love him, and fear him above all, and this is the whole duty of man; and use other creatures in their own place, as creatures should be used. We know not what troubles and difficulties we shall meet with ere long, wherein neither friends nor all the world can do us any good; and then happy shall we be if, with a comfortable heart, we can go to God with David: "Be not far from me, for trouble is near, and there is none to help."[1] If God be then far off from us when trouble is near to us, we may go and cry to him; but his answer will be, "You shall eat the fruit of your own way; you have set at nought all my counsel, and would none of my reproof."[2] You would not draw nigh to me; you shall now call and seek to me, but now you shall not draw nigh to me, you shall not find me. What, then, can our friends do? What can the whole world then supply to us, when sickness comes as "an armed man," and death as a mighty giant, against whom is no resisting; but will we or nill we, away we must be gone? Then to have a God nigh us, to whom we may go as Peter did in the storm, "O Master, save me, I perish,"[3] then to have a friend in heaven, who can for the present guide us by his counsel, and instruct us against Satan's wiles and our deceivable hearts, and be a safe guard to us in the fire and in the water, in the dungeon and when we are

---

1 Psalm 22:11.
2 Proverbs 1:31.
3 Mark 4:35–41.

in the greatest depths of misery to outward sense; though in death, in the shadow of death, and in the valley of the shadow of death, yet can send us such cheerful remembrances of his love, as the cloud shall be scattered, the shadow taken away, and death, an enemy, shall be a friend; nay, a friendly meeting between God and the soul, so as the soul shall triumph in death, and shall delight to die, and desire it: "Lord, now let thy servant depart in peace, for," by the eye of faith, I have "waited for thy salvation."[1] I say, then will the sweetness of this estate of drawing near to God be manifested to us, and then shall we not repent of any labor or travail spent in our lifetime, in the attaining of such a condition.

---

1 Luke 2:29, 30.

Made in the USA
Coppell, TX
18 October 2021